Not Broken®

How to overcome mental health challenges
and unlock your full potential!

Brett Francis

Not Broken:
How to overcome mental health challenges and unlock your full potential!

Copyright © 2016 Brett Francis

Print Edition ISBN: 978-0-9953025-3-2
eBook Edition ISBN: 978-0-9953025-1-8

*ATTENTION CORPORATIONS, ASSOCIATIONS, UNIVERSITIES, COLLEGES AND PROFESSIONAL ORGANIZATIONS: Quantity discounts are available on bulk purchases of this book for educational, inspirational, and gift purposes, or as premiums for increasing memberships. Special book covers or book excerpts can be created to fit specific needs. For more information, please contact Francis Ventures Ltd.: admin@francisventures.ca
or
1-855-910-8255

DEDICATION

To my spouse
*Thank you for loving me for who I really am
and for what I used to think were my weaknesses and flaws*

To Matthew Teulon
You will always be in my heart

To Gloria and Mark Teulon
*I will always be unhappy about losing Matt,
but I will never be unhappy that I've had the privilege
of becoming closer to you*

To my dad
*For showing me the way and being there,
even if you didn't always agree with me*

ACKNOWLEDGMENTS

This is my first book and I have been very blessed to have such a great support system. Countless individuals read through my manuscripts and were very helpful with their feedback. As a first time author, there was much that I did not know but I made it to completion with the feedback and support of my friends, family and colleagues.

The first manuscript I brought to my publisher was a mess and I was surprised he could get through the first chapter let alone the entire manuscript. Instead, he gave me positive and constructive feedback.

I also had a great editor and the second manuscript was the first that I brought to her. She was very knowledgeable, helpful and was a great mentor for writing this book. Quite frankly, I'm surprised she didn't pull her hair out during the process.

This book has been improved by Jeanne Martinson, Cathy Giasson and Bayleigh Napper.

A special acknowledgement to my spouse who read and heard about this book since the day that I started. Also for the emotional support through the process, especially when I became overwhelmed or frustrated.

Lastly, to you who are reading this: Thank you. I hope that you find the book educational, insightful and enjoyable!

DISCLAIMER

I am not a doctor, nutritionist or any other type of medical professional certified by any professional regulatory body or agency. I do not provide medical or psychological counselling.

I do not advise you on medication but promote the benefits of exercise and proper nutrition. You are solely responsible for seeking appropriate medical advice. Do not make any changes to your diet, medication or exercise regime without consulting a certified medical professional.

This book is solely to share my experience for general mental health awareness and inspiration. What works for me with my diagnoses, medical or natural may not work for you.

TABLE OF CONTENTS

FROM THE AUTHOR

I spent most of my life feeling broken wondering what was wrong with me, left unaccepted and alone. I have struggled with mental health and disabilities for the greater part of my life. I lived to learn that this doesn't have to be disabling and activated a power that I may not have found without those challenges. Now I share my empowerment and experiences with others to educate others, stop the stigma and give others that are struggling confidence in their own challenges and to feel comfortable in their own shoes for who they truly are.

1

Introduction

People with mental health challenges and disabilities are not broken and do not need to be fixed. One in four people will struggle with mental illness at some point in their life. For some it will be situational, such as depression after a divorce, job loss, or even being diagnosed with a serious disease like cancer. But for others, mental health challenges and disabilities will be a struggle for life.

One in five people will struggle with mental health (43.8M people the US and 7.17 in Canada)! 80% of left with no or insufficient treatment.

Mental health is the cause of 1/3 of disability claims. 1M US employees (500,000 Canadian employees) miss work every day

> *20% of people will experience mental illness in their lifetime*

due to mental health or workplace stress. Economic loss due to mental health in America $193.2 billion and $10 billion in Canada per annum. Mental health illness and disorder occurrences are higher than breast cancer, lung cancer and heart disease combined! Considering these drastic numbers, you would think that there would be sufficient awareness, education, support and tools for those who struggle. But there aren't.

Mental health barriers are a common challenge yet are under-recognized and overlooked by society and our government. There's inadequate government and private insurance coverage. Nor are there sufficient social support programs for those with mental health challenges and disabilities such as intellectual and cognitive disabilities.

It's easy to understand why mental health and disability challenges are so neglected and put on the back burner. Mental health comes with many misconceptions and myths such as: mental illnesses aren't real illnesses, mental illness is a poor excuse for bad behaviour, people with mental illness are violent and dangerous, you can't recover from mental illness and people with mental illness are weak and can't handle stress. The least of these is that mental illness is invisible – we simply cannot see it like we can see a physical injury or physical disability.

Society, workplaces, government and professionals need to work at creating more mental health awareness, education and support. Isn't it time that we began to work more effectively at awareness, education and support for this neglected but obvious issue?

Do Professionals Help?

There are many types of educated professionals in this field – clinical psychologists, counsellors and psychiatrists have studied how to help people that struggle with mental health challenges. I have seen over 20 of these people personally, none of whom were of any significant benefit. I was simply told that something was wrong with me and how to fix it with a prescription.

Most people with mental health barriers or disabilities feel extremely uncomfortable or intimidated when they see a certified professional. Will the professional understand their struggles? They ask themselves. Will they be judgemental?

Why do mental health and disabilities hold a special place in my heart?

First of all, I've been through it. When I was six years old, I was diagnosed with Tourette's syndrome and ADHD. When I was 17, I was re-diagnosed with the same two conditions as well as anxiety, panic disorder and OCD (Obsessive Compulsive Disorder). Secondly, I lost one of my best friends in 2011 to suicide. Thirdly, mental health barriers and disabilities run in my family; my father, brother and numerous cousins.

School

I was a very poor performer in school, 'mercy' passed in almost every subject. Today, I'm a successful businessperson, yet I almost failed high school. I have very little post-secondary education and needed a tutor for the small courses that I took after high school. It wasn't that I could only achieve as a poor performer. I received poor grades because I didn't try.

I simply learn a different way than how the school curriculum is designed, with it's one template of courses with the same assignments, reading and expectations of each student. It's a cookie cutter curriculum and I am not a confectionary baker. I am an extremely smart individual. I just needed to implement the most effective learning methods that work for me – which might not be for everyone else.

Society

Society has taught parents to take their hyperactive children to a doctor and in a one hour appointment the children are diagnosed with ADHD and are prescribed a medication, often without further research or investigation.

Part of being a normal kid without ADHD is being hyper. I was energetic and bouncing off the walls. (Even though I did have

ADHD). I can't stress enough how much this issue needs to be researched and understood prior to diagnosing and medicating. I have seen many kids become like zombies on medications; not energetic, disinterested in exciting things, disconnected where their entire personalities change.

A friend from high school had severe ADHD, was extremely hyper and impulsive. His parents put him on Ritalin in grade ten and he ceased to be the same person. Not only did he seem like a zombie, but he lost interest in the activities and fun sports he used to love. This was the most common drug for ADHD when I was in high school and frequently had the same side effects my friend experienced.

Understanding mental health and disabilities

Research in mental health and disabilities needs to be done to figure out what the specifics are and to gain a strong understanding of the issue prior to diagnoses. This way, finding natural or medical treatment options will be easier and more effective. Many people get worse due to medicating too soon or rushing into other forms of treatment before they have enough knowledge and understanding.

Have you ever seen or heard of anti-depressants causing a worsening of depression or suicidal thoughts? These and other side effects such as agitation, irritability, anxiety, nausea weight gain, and insomnia are common with almost every anti-depressant. A one-hour intake with a professional isn't enough time to determine and diagnose a person's anatomy and chemical balance. For me, a psychiatrist is only a well-informed starting point.

The brain works in miraculous ways and it's very complex and fascinating. The smallest detail can trigger a symptom: a vitamin deficiency, a specific social situation, a death in the family, poor nutrition, lack of exercise or proper sleep, an abusive relationship. These triggers are specific conditions which can be diagnosed in an appointment with a medial professional.

I was medicated from seven years of age until I was 17. Ten years is a long time.

I've been off medication since I was 18. I do much better without it now that I understand my mental health and disabilities.

No one understands what it's like to be in another's mind. Every single person is different. People who experience mental health challenges and disabilities themselves can usually relate to others who are experiencing the same challenges. However, trying to explain mental health and disabilities to someone who doesn't understand can be very exhausting. Trying to explain anxiety to a person who is without anxiety or worry can be like talking to a brick wall, especially when they minimize or discount your reality with comments such as, "well just don't be anxious" or "it's stupid to be anxious about that." It doesn't work like that. A person can't just decide to not be anxious or depressed. If we had a choice we would have stopped it by now.

> *The only way to overcome mental health barriers and disabilities is to truly understand them yourself. Take the time to get to know yourself and your mental health and disability then don't be ashamed of who you are!*

Although it's difficult and stressful to help someone understand who doesn't experience it first hand, it is not impossible. In my experience, even when you're speaking with someone who can relate. Each person experiences different symptoms and challenges, so we can never completely understand exactly what the other person is experiencing. But we can certainly be supportive.

> *You rule your mental health and disability, it does NOT rule you! You are not it!*

You are worth your own time and understanding. Spend time with yourself and take the time to create self-awareness to overcome your barriers. Have patience to get to know yourself with mental health and disabilities. Don't be ashamed. Mental health challenges and disabilities don't have to be disabling.

What will this book do for you?

This book will help you understand your barriers and help you accept who you are by using the simple approaches that I have used for myself. In the following chapters, I explain the importance of understanding your mental health and disabilities by reading and learning about them. If you choose to see medical professionals, make sure you see them multiple times before diagnosis. Confirm by reading on your own and seeing other professionals. Each person's mental health and disabilities are more complicated than many medical professionals make them out to be. There is not just one solution or medication.

I wrote this book not only out of my deep passion to help, encourage and inspire others, but also to raise awareness, education and support for mental health and disabilities. I hope that the contents of this book will prevent others from going through the hardships that I went through.

As I wrote this book, I asked myself, "do I regret any of my past?" No I do not. I admit there are experiences that I am not proud of and I would never make those choices again. I've been through some very difficult situations, but I wouldn't change them because they define the person that I have become. I wouldn't be sharing my story and writing this book had I not been through those hardships.

2

My Story

My name is Brett Francis. I'm 26 years old. When I was six years old, I was diagnosed with Tourette's syndrome and ADHD. When I was 17, I was re-diagnosed with the same two conditions, plus OCD, anxiety and panic disorder.

In 2012, I was involved in two motor vehicle accidents and suffe r with severe chronic pain syndrome from a neck injury.

I'm a business owner with multiple endeavours: property management, real estate investing, real estate investment coaching, and professional speaking. I am a radio and TV host, a coach and consultant, seminar/webinar leader, workplace mental health consultant, author, and creator of a mental health clothing line.

I love being a volunteer, particularly for the Telemiracle and Kinette Foundation. Th ey assist people with special needs through an annual 20 hour telethon. 2016 was my sixth TeleMiracle. I also fundraise for the American and Canadian Mental Health Associations and am endorsed by them as a mental health advocate.

The things that are most important to me are my life partner, my family, my dog, my two horses, my businesses, my health and my fitness.

Growing up

I have one younger brother, Keifer, who is two years younger than I. Keifer is an amazing young man. When I was five and my brother was three, our parents divorced and we moved every week. We had one week with mom, one week with dad, one week with mom, one week with dad, and so on. Those were hard years for my brother and I. We had to separate our favourite toys and clothes between each household and switch the schedule every week with school. This was exhausting. Dad was self-employed and usually picked us up from school and mom worked as a manager and usually made us walk.

My mom and dad didn't get along too well for the first few years and Keifer and I were often in the middle of their arguments and disagreements. Even though each household was a stable place by itself, going back and forth offered little stability and was overwhelming. This is where it all started for me.

The divorce was tough. I felt like my parents didn't love us anymore because they were always arguing about us and not considering our feelings. I felt like there was a problem with me and that I wasn't good enough for them to stay together. A few years after the divorce, I realized that my parents weren't getting back together. I began to rebel and argue just to get attention. I felt lost.

Any attention was good. I was confused and tired going one week at dad's then one week at mom's. I didn't quite understand why I had to have separate things at each place and I wanted it to stop. I wanted to be at one place with both of my parents together or even with just one of them full-time. Eventually I was with my dad full-time.

Tourette's Syndrome

My symptoms started when I was five. The grunting started and then got louder, developing into a yell. When this started happening in class, my teachers called my parents, asking what was wrong with me. After the grunting and yelling began I developed facial tics with my eyebrows, lips and ears, eye rolling and touching movements where I did circles with my hands and touched/tapped others. In Grade 2 my parents would come to my class to sit with me. Each time I had a tic, they would try to stop me. I couldn't stop the tics and was moved to the back of the class to sit with my parents. I felt like an outcast. I felt different. Why did I do all of this and other kids didn't?

Throughout my middle school and high school years, my Tourette's intensified, peaking in puberty. I didn't handle this well. People yelled to make fun of me, telling me to "Stop that!"

Most people have no idea how hard it is to stop doing something that they have absolutely no control over. When you try to stop with all of your might, and concentration, your symptoms drastically increase and the outburst is stronger. It's extremely frustrating when others tell you to stop having tics because you can't. No matter how much you tell others that you can't, they still tell you to stop. I have broken down in tears many times when this has happened because when the tics are happening, stress and anxiety make them worse and someone telling you to stop ramps up your stress and anxiety and then your tics get even worse so they're telling you to stop more.

> *One of the hardest things I ever had to go through was having others tell me to 'stop' doing my tics. That's possibly the worst feeling in the world to have someone tell you to stop something that you have absolutely zero control over.*

The way that I can explain Tourette's is like carrying a reloading time bomb where the intervals of explosion have no pattern, time consistency, or known blast capability. It is set to go off at any time or place. You know that you're carrying it which makes you nervous, but you still have to go on trying to live your life. So throughout the day, it goes off. You never know when. You never know how bad or what kind of explosion you're going to get this time. No one can carry the bomb for you. No one can diffuse it in time before it explodes. The threat never goes away.

You feel like you have this constant weight and worry on your shoulders. Just before the bomb goes off, you can feel it happening but you can't stop it. You try to duck for cover where people can't see or hear you. The more you try to stop or resist it, the worse the bomb explodes. When it finally explodes you feel a relief, but as soon as that relief is over the bomb resets with yet another unknown timer.

Anxiety and worry exacerbates tics and tics exacerbate anxiety and worry so it feels like you can just never get a break. I still have days where I'm so exhausted from my tics that I just want to snap because I can't make it stop and all I want it just five minutes of peace.

I was embarrassed and ashamed or my Tourette's, I was the only person I ever knew with Tourette's. Why couldn't anyone else have Tourette's? I was alone and an outcast, and screwed up. All I wanted was to make my tics go away for good. I skipped classes, avoiding people and public places.

Wherever I was, I had tics and people looked at me with disgusted looks. The looks that people gave me caused some of the worst feelings and thoughts I have ever had about myself. They looked at me with a look that said, "what the heck is wrong with you?" I often got asked if I was on drugs. Others thought I was high and twitching from hard drugs. One of my bullies made nicknames for me in high school. They called me 'twitch' or 'druggy.' For at least two years, whenever I would walk down the hall I could count on a fellow student calling out these nicknames.

Every time that someone looked at me with that look or called me those names, my self-confidence went down.

Before I knew it, I was in grade nine, depressed and without any self-confidence. I couldn't trust anyone. I was uncomfortable going out in public and to school. I hated my Tourette's and had come to the point where I considered taking my life. I was insecure, overwhelmed, physically and mentally exhausted, wound up and ready to snap. I felt completely controlled by my Tourette's. It was overpowering and devastating. My Tourette's defined me. I was lost losing touch of who I was.

I finally met someone else with Tourette's when I was 26. It was so exciting. We asked each other about our tics and I could finally relate to someone about my Tourette's. We talked for several hours the first time we met. At first I was unsure if I was comfortable disclosing my diagnoses because he was very abrupt, he came right out and asked if I had Tourette's. I said, "yes," wondering what his comment would be. When he said, "I have Tourette's too!" I told him I didn't believe him. I couldn't see any tics. He started telling me about his tics and asking me if I've ever had tics like that before. He described to me how his tics felt and I paused. I screamed out, "*You have Tourette's!*" in an ecstatic voice. I was so excited and we ended up laughing about tics that we each have had throughout our life. For the first time, I had been able to relate to someone who genuinely understood what Tourette's was.

School and Bullying

I was bullied during every year of grade school and high school. I was even bullied through my post-secondary courses and I still get judged and laughed at today.

This was and can still be a really hard thing for me. Feeling like an outsider and loner with no purpose or use where no one accepts you, is an awful feeling.

In school, I had students pretend to be my friends but behind my back would yell "Tourette's" or other demeaning names. I was shoved in lockers, had my school supplies stolen, and setup to be humiliated. I did not feel safe anywhere in my school. I neglected the classes I loved to avoid embarrassment or shame.

I was not a strong student. I felt stupid because I couldn't understand the textbooks, writing and reading. I was mercy-passed for most years. The teachers just thought that I wasn't paying attention, which eventually I wasn't. No matter how hard

I tried, I could never get anywhere. I felt it was pointless. I was on medication for Tourette's that made me extremely drowsy enough to sleep through many of my classes.

School really never got better for me. I take the odd course here and there now but even those are difficult to get through and motivated for. Bullying took me away from everything – school, work and activities. I already struggled with school and considered myself stupid but the bullying stripped away my effort and interest. I was depressed all the time and embarrassed about who I was. I over-focused in an attempt to figure out how I could *not be me*.

When I was diagnosed with Tourette's, my parents told me to be open with everyone and tell them. They promised that everyone would be understanding, so I did. I regretted telling anyone because people weren't understanding. They were judgemental and malicious, constantly teasing and asking what's wrong with me. I was furious with my parents that they made me tell everyone and that they shared my diagnosis. From that point forward, I resented my parents, a feeling that continued for the better part of my school years. I felt isolated, dreading being in school around others, being tormented by the other kids. I was helpless and felt like I couldn't confide in anyone.

My dad and I moved us to Regina once I had completed grade 11. He was expanding his businesses and brought me with him because he felt I needed a new start. He knew how hard things were for me and it was hard for him to see me come home far after curfew drunk or high. It was hard for him to see me bullied and struggle with friends the way that I did. This move was a large contributor to my turning point. When my dad and I moved to Regina when I was 16, I did not tell anyone at my new school. Things were much better for me. By this time my tics had become less intense and noticeable. I still had the typical high school drama with friends and boys, but did not get bullied for my Tourette's. This was such a relief. No one knew that I had Tourette's.

Family

Mental health barriers and learning disabilities are hereditary in my family: ADHD, anxiety, chronic depression, and bipolar disorder. Every second member of my family has some degree of mental illness or disability. I am the only one with Tourette's Syndrome.

I was a rotten and rebellious kid. I broke the rules, stole from others, ignored my chores, and didn't listen to anything my parents had to say. When they said no to me – I threw temper tantrums. I argued and had to have things my way. I played my parents against each other taking advantage of their divorced parent guilt. I used manipulation and guilt. I did this because I resented them for telling everyone I had Tourette's.

I felt like an outcast to my family and that I didn't fit in. My cousins were getting educations, having stable jobs, getting married, having kids. I was nowhere near any of those things, which made me feel disappointed in myself. I was a screw up and hopeless. My dad kicked me out a few times. The first time I was 15 and I went to live with my high school boyfriend in a trailer park. We smoked, drank and partied every night. Eventually, I moved back in with my dad for another few months before I was kicked out again. I lived with yet another high school boyfriend in a junky apartment. I was kicked out of my father's house at least five times before I was 18, and each time I moved to a different place. I felt my family was disappointed in who I was and didn't accept me, that they wouldn't support or be there for me.

A few years ago, I read an article that said rebellious children are more likely to be entrepreneurs and successful because they're willing to take risks. I of, course, shared the article with my parents and said, "See, there was a method to my madness!"

No matter what I did, even if my dad didn't agree with it or support my decisions, he was always there for me. He was always making sure that I was okay. I feel very fortunate to have had the great father that I did. Without him, I probably wouldn't be where

I am today or pulled out of my rock bottom. Once I really started making an effort, the rest of my family and I became closer.

Friends

From the age of 12, I had one good friend. She is still my friend today. She went to a different middle and high school, she knew I got bullied but couldn't do much about it being in different schools. She was the only one who really truly had my back and didn't judge me. She struggles with anxiety and depression so we were drawn close because of that.

The other friends that I thought that I had weren't really friends at all. They would talk about me behind my back, invite me to parties to make fun of me, say that they were not my friend when in front of others, and call me names. I was invited to be someone's friend or girlfriend so they could hurt me or make fun of my Tourette's or because they had made a bet with someone. I soon became suspicious and untrusting of others' intentions.

The people in my life that went out of their way to purposely hurt me because of my disability were never-ending. This made me feel worthless, depressed and always wondering if I was a bad person and how I caused others to think that. I started to believe the mean things people would say.

I would pretend to be sick almost every morning so I didn't have to go to school. This is one of the ways I rebelled and argued with my parents. I purposely missed most of grade nine through eleven before my dad and I moved to Regina for grade 12.

I felt like there was no one I could rely on or trust and that everyone was out to hurt or bully me. I became paranoid thinking anyone who spoke to me was just trying to get some sort of leverage to bully me or to start a rumour about me. At one point I had ten rumours about me going around the school, all being untrue. Most of them were unrelated to my Tourette's: sleeping around, having unprotected sex, having Down Syndrome, being on drugs, having fake physical features and cosmetic surgery. People seemed to take jabs at me wherever they could with whatever they could, so you can see now how I became paranoid. I wouldn't let anyone in. It was awful. Every day being me was crap. I hated it and wanted to be anyone else. I wasn't popular, but even the unpopular students wouldn't talk to or be seen with me. Anyone seen with me was bullied for being with me. I was completely alone in high school and skipped over 70% of grade 9-11.

Medication

I was medicated for Tourette's Syndrome and/or OCD for over ten years of my life.

I was first on an anti-psychotic drug which I found out a few years ago should not have been prescribed for Tourette's Syndrome and that it can actually make tics worse. This is the drug that made me sleep during my classes when I did actually go to school. I fell asleep everywhere and could never get enough sleep. I was always exhausted. It gave me this weird looking up thing where I would roll my eyes into the back of my head and no matter what I did, I could not get them to come down. This was frustrating. It disabled me from doing anything even at home. It was also very painful. I resorted to flicking my head to try and get it to stop and switch my concentration.

When I was 17, I stopped that drug and went on a medication my new psychiatrist prescribed me for a few months. It also made me tired, but not as severely as the previous drug. The withdrawals from the first drug that I had been on since I was ten lasted months and put me into depression, increased my anxiety and gave me some extremely unpleasant physical side effects.

The second drug gave me some of the rarest side effects listed for the drug: depression, anxiety, ringing of the ears, saliva and body fluid color changes, skin redness and rashes. They were both physical and mental, and very unpleasant. I had to stop this drug cold turkey because of the extreme side effects. I couldn't get into my psychiatrist for a few weeks. The withdrawals from this second drug were even worse than the first drug. I was sick to my stomach. I was irritable, drowsy, emotional and anxious. I went to see my psychiatrist as these withdraw symptoms subsided. He recommended a medication for OCD because Tourrette's can be aggravated by OCD and anxiety. He figured if we could get the OCD and anxiety under control, then my tics would decrease in frequency and severity.

I went on this new medication for a couple of weeks and started having panic attacks every night. I felt like I was having a heart attack or couldn't breathe – and would end up in the hospital. My psychiatrist recommended that I go off this medication cold turkey, so I did. The withdrawal symptom that was the most prominent from this third drug was the feeling like I had stuck my finger in an electrical outlet. My whole body got a large electric jolt. At first, it happened every few seconds. I couldn't function and was completely disabled. This frequency lasted for three very long weeks and finally tapered off.

My psychiatrist finally recommended one more medication but this time for ADHD, to help focus and anxiety. This drug was the easiest one on my system. I really didn't notice anything for a couple months, good or bad. After three months on the drug, I started to gain weight. It was only ten pounds, but the gain made me feel very badly about my body considering I was eating healthy and being active. Because I didn't notice any real positive side effects of the drug, I decided to stop.

By this point, I felt completely discouraged and like a lost cause. No medication had helped me. I was disappointed that medication would not make my Tourrette's and other diagnoses improve.

Since that time, I have not been on any medication. Medications have bee very troublesome and bothering. I felt I was just given prescriptions and then told to go home. No time invested just that a medication would fix me. I felt like the doctors didn't want to help me and didn't care but just wanted me to take another cure without any other methods.

Alcohol and Drugs

Half way through grade nine, I couldn't bear to go to school anymore. I couldn't live with myself. I hated myself and didn't know how anyone could like me; I even started to doubt my own friendships. When I was forced by my parents to go to school, I resorted to drugs and alcohol. I always found some older boy to 'pull' alcohol or cigarettes for me. I hid a mickey of hard liquor in my locker and went to drink from it throughout the day. When I got home from school, I would tell my dad that I was doing my homework, but I was texting other friends that I could go and get drunk or high with later. I would go out almost every night after supper and come home past curfew. I didn't even like the people that I went out with, but I could escape reality with drugs and alcohol. I never even liked being drunk or high, I just drank or used more so those negative feelings went away. Drugs usually made my anxiety worse. Marijuana would put me into an instant panic attack, so I went for the harder stuff. I wasn't okay being the person that I was, but getting drunk or high made me forget about all of that. I drank and did drugs because it was a temporary escape from who I was. For a while I didn't have to worry about being me because the substances made me not care. It felt amazing to not be me for the short time that it lasted, so I did more drugs because I wanted to escape from myself even more.

When I moved to Regina, I stopped doing drugs and alcohol out of a need to escape or numb myself. I partied like a typical teen, but was with friends. As soon as we left Swift Current, I no longer felt the need to get drunk or high because I didn't have to be so embarrassed and ashamed about being me. This time, I was around people who actually liked me. I figured they liked me because I didn't tell them I had Tourette's. Seeing the difference in the way people treated me with and without knowing about my Tourette's caused me to feel even more ashamed and embarrassed. I never wanted to tell anyone again so when my symptoms showed up, I always had an excuse: I tripped, I have hiccups, my foot slipped…

Relationships and Jobs

I wasn't very stable. In fact, I was extremely instable. I couldn't keep a job for more than a couple of weeks. I was always job searching. I procrastinated all the time. I couldn't get anything done, nor did I have any interest in doing anything important. I had no follow through, didn't believe in myself. I felt sorry for myself but didn't do anything about it. I didn't think that I was worthy of a good job and that everyone would just fire me because of my Tourette's. I got fired from numerous jobs thanks to my Tourette's. (*I didn't tell them that I had it and couldn't explain my behaviour*) That made it very hard for me to even find interest in working. I would always find an excuse to quit.

I couldn't make my rent payments. I got myself into thousands of dollars of debt, and all before I was 19 years old. I would always guilt my dad into giving me money to pay my bills and then I wouldn't actually pay my bills.

I also couldn't keep a boyfriend. I didn't trust anyone. I searched for and amplified flaws. I got dumped a lot in high school because of my Tourette's as the boys eventually didn't want to be seen associating with me. I had some relationships where they wanted to be with me, but just not for anyone to know. I just needed to keep quiet about it. I was in a lot of physically and emotionally abusive relationships. When I was 15, I was sexually abused. I was set up by two of my 'best friends'. They thought it would be a good prank. They locked my in my room with a boy that I liked and held their ears up to the door threatening me. They thought we could just laugh and be friends. This incident is where most of my relationship instability and lack of trust came from. I felt like something was taken from me and figured that I had no right to respect and I wasn't worthy to make my own choices. Other students threatened to start rumours about me at school if I told anyone about this incident. I was already bullied enough at school and couldn't bear the thought of more bullying. I lost trust in everyone, even my closest family. I felt like something was wrong with me, why did this happen to me and why do people not want to be my friends and want to hurt me? Something must be seriously wrong with me, but what? I felt betrayed and confused that my so-called 'friends' would want to do this to me. They thought that it was funny, and at my expense. I thought everyone was out to get me and that I was worthless and a loser that everyone hated. I had never been so hurt in my life, this had topped all of the bullying that I went through. This is when I started to experiment with drugs and alcohol. Shortly after this happened to me, I started contemplating taking my own life because it obviously wasn't worth anything to anyone else.

Miscarriage

Complete rock bottom for me came when I was 19 years old. I was pregnant with a baby boy. This was an unexpected pregnancy. I was not ready to be a mother, but I was going to have the child. At four months into my pregnancy, I lost the child.

Shortly after my miscarriage and the depression that followed it, I left my abusive relationship with my baby's father and my other poor choice of friends.

I lost my sense of being and felt like a nobody. I didn't know who I was anymore. I couldn't understand why my boyfriend hadn't been there for me in the hospital and that my life meant nothing. When they told me I lost the baby at the hospital, it felt like someone had ripped my heart out from my chest. I had to be induced to go into labour and had over a 16 hour labour for this four month old boy. Not only did I lose my child, but I had to do it all alone. My boyfriend at the time was cheating on my while I was in the hospital losing our son. My dad came to visit me and make sure I was okay, but I spend the rest of the three days in the hospital by myself – alone.

When I passed the baby, they asked me if I wanted to hold him. I said "no". I couldn't bear the thought of him not being alive in my arms. I regretted this decision every single waking moment for quite a while. I felt like a cruel, awful and disgusting person. The hospital put him on a little blanket with a pin and glass teddy bear ornament, took a picture of him and gave it to me in a folder that said, "My first born." I cried myself to sleep every night for months. I had lost everything and the floor had been taken out from underneath my feet. I was not ready to be a mother but that didn't mean I wanted my baby taken from me.

It took me well over a year to mend my heart and forgive myself. I had somehow blamed myself for the loss of my child. I was on a mental health leave, not working or doing anything except for laying in bed, eating and crying.

Depression

Throughout my life, I have struggled with very severe situational depression. The two major episodes were after my friends set me up to be sexually abused and after my miscarriage. After my sexual abuse just after my fifteenth birthday, I started cutting myself on my wrists and inner thighs. Initially this was to give myself physical pain to escape the emotional pain; I would rather have unimaginable physical pain than the emotional pain I was experiencing. I had scars and scabs on my wrists and thighs and then tried new places on my body that hasn't been cut.

At first it was just cutting. When I couldn't cause myself enough physical pain to escape the emotional pain, I started to contemplate taking my own life. No one would care if I was gone. I felt disgusted with who I was, alone, confused, overwhelmed and abandoned.

There were several nights when I had laid out a number of different pill bottles with a big glass of water. I planned to take them and cry myself to sleep – or get so drunk or high that I would fall asleep.

The reason why I did not follow through with taking my own life is my younger brother, Keifer. We argued like every brother and sister, but Keifer was the only person in my life that I did not resent. He was always there and I never felt like he judged me. He always listened and told me that things would be okay, he never left or betrayed me. There was a part of me that wanted to live up to be a big sister that he could look up to rather than acting like a big brother to me.

I was somehow able to pull through each time, but it took time and help in each instance. I went through smaller depression phases with Tourette's, my school years with friends and bullying, relationship abuse, lack of employment and purpose, and my miscarriage. Until I was 21, my life was an emotional roller coaster, up and down. I often was not okay with the person that I was.

I would have given anything to be anyone else to get rid of my Tourette's, ADHD, anxiety, OCD and panic disorder. I was just plain screwed up and everything was wrong with me. Every counsellor or psychologist that I went to made me feel this way too. I denied that I had those diagnoses and lied to myself that I didn't have them too (*even Tourette's*). I was always trying to fit in yet I never could, feeling like an outcast for a very large portion of my life. I continuously fought my diagnoses, trying to live without them. I couldn't stand who I was. I had no sense of purpose and just plain hated life and everyone in it.

Oddly enough, I still felt the need for acceptance from people because I was insecure and tried to impress others. I did things out of peer pressure that I didn't actually want to do and that sometimes put me into unsafe environments. I couldn't be alone with myself and needed the attention from others in an attempt to avoid being who I was. I let others define me.

I never seemed to be happy with the person that I was. I was always ashamed. I had no purpose in life and often felt like I had nothing to live for. Nobody cared about me or would notice that I was gone and sometimes I contemplated taking my own life.

Anxiety, OCD and Panic Disorder

If I was ever given a choice of only one diagnosis that I could get rid of, it would surprisingly *not* be Tourette's. I would have gotten rid of my anxiety. Anxiety, OCD and panic disorder are not easy diagnoses, especially with Tourette's. Tourette's makes them worse and they make Tourette's worse. Medication for Tourette's makes these others worse and medication for these others makes Tourette's worse. The diagnoses flaring up together felt like a downward spiral that I had an extremely hard time managing, I couldn't figure anything out. Every time I thought about how to help myself, my anxiety kicked in and I just wanted to ignore it.

I have anxiety day-to-day. I get anxious even by thinking about what I have to do today. My anxiety used to cripple me because I would start thinking so much. I didn't know where or how to start my days, so I just didn't start them. I missed work, school and activities. I got overwhelmed and felt like there was so much to do even when I had only three things to do. It just felt never ending. I would get anxiety from things not being perfectly organized or counted so I became consumed by organizing things even before I could start doing anything. I could never feel totally organized so spent all of my time organizing rather than actually doing the tasks I needed to complete. My OCD made my anxiety worse and then when I would get anxiety I would have physical symptoms, which led me to panic attacks. I continued in the vicious pattern and could never get things done because I was too worried about organizing them. I searched for years to find task management and note software that made it easier for me. Finally after four years of searching, I found one that was a match. What a breeze and weight off of my shoulders.

It's difficult to explain anxiety if you don't have it. You just can't relate. It's these hectic and overactive thoughts in your brain never stopping that cause you to constantly feel tense and anxious. For me, it's also this gut feeling. I may say, "I am having anxiety." When another person asks why, I say, "I just have anxiety." There is really no rhyme or reason to it, you just get it and most of the time can't explain why. It's this feeling for no reason and it's exhausting.

Of course, stressful and fast paced situations can make it worse. I often feel there is never enough time in a day and I can't get it all done – even if I only have three things on my to do list. That's also part of being a business owner and I made a conscious choice to have that lifestyle. I get overwhelmed thinking about the things I have to and want to do. I wonder how I am going to do it or get the process done. It is pointless worry and I know that. I get so overwhelmed with details that I have a very hard time computing them and often feel like there should be smoke coming out my ears for thinking so much. I can't fall asleep at night because my mind never shuts off. I've got to watch a cartoon or read so I can nod off.

Anxiety if very frustrating because it can get worse at any time and for any reason. It never really goes away – your mind just keeps spinning. Your mind is never at rest and there is no switch that you can use to shut it down. Your anxiety doesn't care where you are or who you are with. Even when you're sleeping, you dream about your thoughts. This anxiousness is like having five of your own voices in your head, constantly trying to talk over each other. It's going 24/7, it's like your brain is on a constant dose of speed. Anxiety makes me feel disconnected, edgy and out of control.

I get anxiety every night at the same time. I get an adrenaline rush that takes its toll on my body. I still get that anxiety at least ten times a day or more. Although I haven't gotten rid of my anxiety, I certainly have learned to manage well. I have developed a routine with my anxiety that can make it subside.

Anxiety and OCD are exhausting because they make you feel like you just can't rest or get a break. Anxiety is both mentally and physically exhausting. It plays a role in every area of my life. My OCD rituals have been extremely disabling, and I often spend more time on the rituals than the actual tasks themselves. Your brain and body are always on and sometimes you just want to be able to take a step back and 'chill' without having to feel like you need to get something done. I've been 'on' since I was in Grade one, sometimes going 36 hours without sleep.

I am always tense and need to learn ways to get an "active" break. I'm an active relaxer so I go for walks, read a business book to stimulate my mind on a different path, organize the house, go for a drive, go run errands, go see my horses or shoot my bow. I have learned that trying to force myself to relax the way many others relax actually stresses me out more and makes my anxiety peak.

ADHD

ADHD affects me in quite a few ways. When I was younger, I sucked at school even when I put effort in. I was very messy and disorganized. I procrastinated with everything that I didn't have interest in. When I did have interest in the work, it was short lived and I didn't stick with it. I couldn't keep my attention on things for long periods of time. I often tried to multi-task and then forgot about certain tasks that I started. I had poor prioritising and would continue to do non-important things and leave the important ones out. To this day, it is difficult for me to stay on task and not get distracted. It's so easy to get distracted by something else.)

Because of my brief attention span, I have an awful memory. If I don't write things down, the moment I forget about them they may be gone forever. Or I remember when it is no longer important.

In the past, I became bored very easily and quickly. I often quit tasks minutes in, quit jobs after a few days and quit activities after a few weeks. Sometimes I would sit for 10 hours and 'work', yet when I looked at my to do list at the end of these hours, nothing was done. Things were forgotten because I tried to multi-task. I skipped between 20 different things, not finishing any of them. I also had a difficult time focusing on any one task for more than 20 minutes. I have learned to give myself a quick five minute break after I actually stay focused for a while. When this happens it's much easier to get things done and I start tasks easier, where before I would just procrastinate because I was dreading the tasks and focus.

The "H" (*hyperactivity part*) caused me to be very hyper and easily excitable, but also easily discouraged, upset or stressed. I had problems with anger and was impatient. Everything often was an emergency and I just couldn't wait. I had a problem listening and tended to talk A LOT, talk over people and blurt things out impulsively. I also had a hard time not saying inappropriate things that I hadn't thought through before I opened my mouth. I was very impulsive with my decisions, including quitting jobs and spending money. I didn't stick with sports or jobs most of the time because I was bored easily and couldn't stay focused. Either that or I was discouraged because I wasn't instantly the best. I didn't have the patience to learn and take time to improve.

I often used to be late or not show up for things. I had no sense of time and frustrated many people around me. It was like "Murphy's Law" (*anything that can happen will or anything that can go wrong will*) because I would often not focus on tasks. I would decide to get focused at the worst times, minutes before I had to be somewhere, "just another minute," I would tell myself and after 20 minutes of crunching out the task that I couldn't do for the past week, I would look at the clock and realize that I was going to be late.

Chronic pain

I have been living with severe chronic pain from a neck and back injury from two motor vehicle accidents, neither that were my fault. I was hit twice in 2012 and was off work for nearly a full year in an attempt to recover. Not only do I have severe chronic pain, but I also suffer with constant headaches that often become migraines that make me nauseous. I would describe chronic pain as debilitating, treacherous, irritating, frustrating, tormenting, and disheartening. It never goes away – I have to learn to live with it and make the best of what I cannot change. I still go to physiotherapy on a regular basis. I also have an exercise and strengthening plan that my physiotherapist advised which I do between appointments.

I found an article a few months ago. It describes chronic pain and hits the head on the nail. Here is a part of the article and a link to the complete piece:

"To the person who thinks chronic pain "can't be that bad."

"I have a friend. A poisonous friend.

When she is angry, she makes my days hell and my nights sleepless. She attacks me when I least expect it, especially if I'm lulled into a sense of security. She follows me everywhere, every day to the point where I truly cannot remember a time that I lived totally out of her clutches.

She is cruel. She cares little for family occasions, first dates, social events and the like. She perhaps forces me to stay home, or she makes sure she is right there with me, ensuring I don't forget her presence for a moment.

She's been a silent witness to some of the most remarkable and agonizing moments of my life.

She's always here.

Her name is Pain.

There are many who live with her, just like me. We do our best to keep on living despite her glowering presence. It doesn't matter how long you live with her, you never become immune to her.

Yes, we learn to continue our lives, even the mundane daily stuff that keeps it "normal." Yes, we smile, laugh and make jokes. We make love, shop and eat, despite the anger it causes her to display, and we relish and appreciate anew the simple joys that take much to remove or lessen.

But let me tell you a secret. It hurts! It never stops. You wake, it hurts. You rest, it hurts. You do some basic physical activity, it hurts. You eat, it hurts.

See, constant and chronic pain isn't something you magically get "immune" to.

You don't get magically used to pain.

Let me tell you another secret.

Normally, pain is your body's sharp and intense warning that something is amiss. You are meant to feel it, and the amount of pain allows you to determine how serious the injury may be. With chronic pain, the pain is no different. It screams at you to notice it. It rends your heart and mind with its incessant demands to be noticed and treated. However, no matter what the pain relief is, unless there is an urgent or acute injury or illness on top of that pain, then the aim of the medical profession is to relieve it to a degree. The aim is not to take away pain. It is not necessarily realistic to do so long-term unless we are palliative. So that's the next secret I have for you. Despite often hefty pain-relieving medications, pain is diminished to the point that we can push through it and attempt normal function, but she is still right there

Here's another secret.

It's rare for someone who lives with pain to actually tell you that she hurts so badly she fights the urge to bash her head against a wall, or scream, or just cry about the unbearable unfairness of it all. While you look on, we protect you from our pain. "Nah, it's fine, just a twinge." "It's OK, I'm just a bit sore." Or the automatic response, "Fine thanks, how are you?"

We learn fast. To tell you of pain, and the misery she brings, often eventually creates anger, resentment, ill-treatment, impatience, and out and out rudeness. At first it's all sympathy. But I don't want that! Empathy! That's what I need.

This is why I protect you. Because to one who hasn't experienced chronic, disabling pain, to show that I hurt appears to diminish me, to be a weakness, a failing. It's humiliating to justify my pain, so I seldom choose to do so.

The best thing that you can do for a friend or loved one who also lives with pain is to realize that pain hurts! If we are exhausted, sore or unwilling to do some activity, it's because we hurt, badly. Even at the moment that you helpfully attempt to change the subject, that hurts, too. When you chatter brightly about your toe or that sore back you had once, you diminish our reality and you diminish your capacity to hold anything nearing empathy for us. Instead, ask what tangible thing you can do to help. Or say truthfully, "I don't know how that must feel, but I'm here if you need me. I believe you. I love you."

Most important, here is the final secret I will share with you.

Pain moved in uninvited. We didn't ask for her or welcome her. She is something inflicted on us entirely against our wishes. So please don't punish us for something we have zero control over. And learn to listen *to us, and hear what may be underneath our "just a bit sore" and "It's OK." That means more than anything.*

– Krissy Purcell

http://themighty.com/2016/04/letter-to-people-who-think-chronic-pain-isnt-that-bad/

How did I change?

Months after my miscarriage, I woke up and had enough. I was sick of being a victim and not enjoying life. Nothing ever went right. I went one step forward and many backwards. Nothing ever happened how I wanted it to. Just as I was getting ahead, everything would fall apart. Until I realized that I was creating this pattern for myself.

My father said that everything in life is a choice – how you feel, how you act, how you react, it's all a choice. At the time I didn't understand how this could be true. How can I choose how somebody else makes me feel? How can I choose the path of my feelings and the path of anything in my life when life just happens? How do I have control over my path? Isn't life already set for me? Doesn't life have a plan for me?

Even though I didn't understand and even though I really didn't believe it I told myself that I deserved better. I started reading books, researching, phoning my dad ten times a day (*which I'm sure he didn't appreciate very much but he was always supportive*). I made lists and tried tactics that I read about. I tried silly and small things and way out there things. There wasn't anything that I wasn't prepared to try. I didn't stick with most of it because of my procrastination. I had anxiety about changing and how I was going to do these things. I felt like I had too much change and self-work to do. I doubted things would ever get better and that I was capable of anything. I didn't think that I would succeed or I deserved to. I was overwhelmed with all these things I wanted to do. I didn't know where to start – so I just didn't start. It seemed easier that way.

When I got overwhelming anxiety, I quit – because changing a lifetime of habits and ways of living didn't happen immediately or provide me with instant gratification. I fell back into my old habits. I realized how unhappy I was so I started doing affirmations that I read about in a book.

An affirmation is when you tell yourself that everything is better than it actually is. So an affirmation is, "I am wealthy," "I am happy," "I have a great life," "I have a great job," even if you don't have those things. See why telling yourself those untruths makes you feel awful? Basically you're lying to yourself. Of course it didn't work because everything I told myself I felt horrible about and didn't believe.

Then I tried declarations. A declaration is something that you tell yourself about your current situation to make yourself feel good about it. A declaration is something like, "I'm working harder towards my goals of having a better job," "I'm putting more time towards being a mother," "I'm working towards being wealthy," "I'm changing my nutrition and exercise to be more fit," "I'm aiming towards having a better lifestyle."

Starting this self-talk and getting into exercising really helped me be able to relax, focus and control my anxiety. I found the things that made me happy and kept on doing them. If something works for me, it may not work for somebody else. I had suggestions from close friends and family that I tried that just didn't work for me, but they worked fantastically for them. I have examples throughout this book as well as a "Techniques and Tools" chapter at the end of the book to help you with some great ideas and things to try.

I reached a point where the scales turned from more negative to more positive in my life. Positive thoughts led to positive words which led to positive actions which led back to positive thoughts. And this continued to an upward cycle. It's a cycle and it's a ripple effect, where each

You ARE worth it! The only true failure is giving up!

positive thing leads to another which leads to another which leads to another, ultimately spiralling upward. Once you tip the scales to 51% of positivity things start to get better, to turn around, and you see the major changes.

I probably started it about 5% positivity and 95% negativity without trust in any other human being. I still have a hard time trusting people. It's once I started to get higher up on the scales from the 5%, where 10% felt good, 15% felt great, 20% felt fantastic – I felt like it couldn't get any better, but I continued to try. I never gave up.

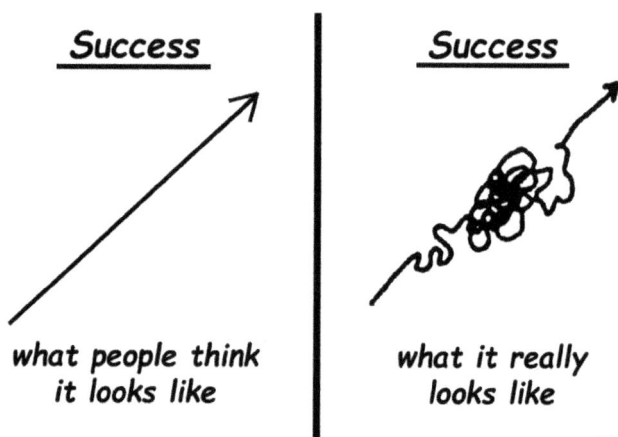

Success

*what people think
it looks like*

Success

*what it really
looks like*

We have to go through unexpected turns, we get thrown curved balls, we get caught up in the mess, but there's still a way through.

There's an image in chapter five that shows the success of people that own multi-million dollar companies and how many times that they failed. The most successful executives in the world and the owners of the Fortune 500 companies say that they have failed up to 10,000 times. That's a lot of failures to reach their goals! Astounding. What does that tell you? It tells me that we need to persevere, that the only true failure is giving up!

Why do I care?

First and foremost – you are worth it. Each and every single person deserves the best possible life that they can have. I saw better for myself… well eventually I did. But it took extreme persistence and energy, plus a good support person. Dealing with mental health and disabilities is absolutely exhausting at times and you feel not only mentally drained but physically as well. It's important to know your limits and to give yourself a break and some quiet "me" time when you get exhausted. If you don't, your symptoms are amplified. I have a very bad habit of working until three or four in the morning. I feel productive then because I have trouble sleeping. However, I know that is the worst time for me to work because not only do I have a hard time thinking straight when my body is exhausted but it takes me ten times longer to do anything! If I do work after 10 or 11pm, I restart my brain activity with little to no chance of sleep.

I didn't have many good friends, but I did have my dad. Most, if not all, of my friends betrayed me at some point or other. I had no friends for the first four years following the end of my abusive relationship. My dad was my everything. I wouldn't be where I am without him. I would still be a victim, not knowing that the things that happened in my life were all a choice. Even though he didn't go through exactly what I was going through, he was still there, and always tried to help. Having people in your life that try to understand you, even if they don't understand you, makes a world of difference – because they care. Let those people in to try to understand and let them be there for you even if they don't understand – because they're trying. I figured out how to use my mental health barriers and disabilities to my advantage and found how they can benefit my life rather than drag me down.

I tried because I was tired of it always being the same negativity and drain. It was exhausting, nothing ever working out. I knew that it was more work to stay the way that I was than to really make an effort to better myself and overcome my barriers.

How did I find and continue to have the strength?

I was tired of my life the way that it was ... not going anywhere. I was self-sabotaging every little ounce of my potential. Many people never do it, yet it's the first and most crucial step to change. You can't change if you don't admit to yourself that you're a victim of things, that you're a victim of yourself.

> *Admitting to yourself that you're a victim is hard.*

Being a victim is not a bad thing, it just means that you have the potential to be better. It's not something you need to be ashamed of. I'm not ashamed to say that I was a victim, because I pulled out of it. It was hard at the time, and it took me at least six months after my rock bottom to admit that I was a victim and that I self-sabotaged my own potential.

Initially I tried to change out of desperation to get away from where I was in life. I was running away from unhappiness and towards hope. Even when I had a negative outlook and things didn't work out, I still wasn't losing anything to try because my life seemed to be way worse not trying. Once I got a taste of the positivity circle and ripple effect and a taste of what it could be like to be happier, prouder and more stable, the want and need for more just kept me going. Very slowly but surely my life started turning around. One positive thought to one positive action leads to more positive. It just continues and you get hooked on it in a positive way.

Hooked on positivity, that's what I am! Hooked on trying to be better, hooked on trying to improve my life, hooked on trying to be happier. I'm already really happy, but I'm always trying to be the best person that I can be every day and I love that.

Finally, there was a point where I became addicted to this optimism and endless effort towards having a better life. Endless effort to be a better person, to help people, to love people, to make people smile. I was addicted to it, and it's contagious. I love being able to make people happy, I love being able to make them smile.

I get happy and excited just by trying to be happy and optimistic, even if things don't work out, even if things fail. I still struggle every day, but those just seem like irritating little hiccups rather than trying to climb a mountain without any rock climbing equipment or hiking tools. Just little hiccups.

I still get irritated about my Tourette's Syndrome, I still get embarrassed about it, but as soon as I walk out to the public place that I'm in or as soon as I take a breath, the irritation and embarrassment are gone. These times are momentary and will never go away, but that's also part of what makes us who we are. I don't wish for my hiccups

The roadblocks and obstacles define who we are. Whether positive or negative, choose to conquer them and make yourself stronger!

to go away, because they continue to make me stronger, they continue to make me grow. If we didn't have challenges or difficulties we wouldn't evolve into better people. I wouldn't change my roadblocks and obstacles for the world. Each time I encounter one, it provides me with a story to share and an opportunity to help someone else conquer theirs!

3

Bullying

Something has caused every person to be where and who they are, good or bad, channelled in a positive or a negative way. It's important not to assume that others' situations are any easier than our own. It's easy to judge someone that exerts their energy in a negative or harsh way.

I have changed the way that I reflect and feel about the people that bullied or wronged me. When I look back, I remind myself that I didn't know what kind of home life the bullies had, for all I know they could have had a worse home life than I did. Oftentimes they had an abusive home life, a bullying sibling, a parent pass away or something else traumatic happen in their life that caused them to be the way that they are.

Bullies can be the people that are bullied the most. People act out of their own insecurities, upbringing and emotions. Negative emotions and insecurities can make people act out of control and not like themselves because often they lose their sense of self from being bullied and don't know how to act or deal with it.

Ways that people that are being bullied themselves may act out:

- Bully others
- Abuse others (*Physical, verbal, emotional or sexual*)
- Lying about others
- Committing crimes: vandalizing, stealing, breaking and entering
- Being overly competitive
- Rude behaviour
- Over polite behaviour
- Isolating themselves
- Being too social
- Being controlling
- Being accusatory and blaming others
- Overly humorous at the expense of others
- Being overly positive, not seeing issues
- Constantly putting themselves down
- Bragging
- Cutting down others' success
- Making excuses
- Not taking responsibility for their actions
- Being a bad loser or poor sport
- Threatening others
- Buying bigger or better material items to impress others (*house, vehicle, clothes*)
- Holding grudges or not forgiving
- Magnifying things out of proportion

If somebody treats me poorly now, I remind myself that I still need to treat them the best that I can, to be a good person towards them – because I don't know what's happening in their life. Maybe they have a mental health barrier or disability that I can't see. Take a step back and pull yourself outside of the situation so you are able to be calm about others' actions and know that they probably don't mean to hurt you.

We judge ourselves way too much, we are our own worst self-critics. I know that if I wake up in the morning and I've got a huge pimple on my forehead, I am panicking. I think about it for the rest of the day, even after I cover it with make-up. I can guarantee that nobody else is worrying about the zit on my forehead, let along notices it at all. We tend to magnify things beyond what they actually are, when really no one else would notice if we didn't say anything.

4

Why Do We Care So Much About What Others Think?

I believe that psychologists, psychiatrists, and other professionals tend to diagnose too quickly without looking at specific underlying issues or current situations. They spend an hour with a person and have a diagnosis to 'fix.' We don't need to be fixed; we are not broken.

Our society has based these diagnoses on clinical studies that do not search for underlying issues that could be making a difference – like vitamin deficiencies, nutrition, situational stress or physical health. Little in these studies is an understanding that each individual is different and that one mental health barrier isn't experienced the same for everyone. This isn't the fault of the curriculum for psychologists and psychiatrists, or of those psychologists and psychiatrists themselves. This is the fault of the lack of understanding and awareness that we have about mental health in our society today. People really don't understand these issues unless they experience them. Even then, each individual is significantly different.

There is not enough help from governments, health systems or support groups and the wait to see a professional in a government program is extremely long. When I went through it, I felt like just a number that had finally risen to the top of the list.

In my experience, these professionals are the ones who helped me the least. There aren't many clinics for mental health. Most support groups and health system programs lack the support that people with mental health barriers and disabilities need and the cost for private professionals is substantial. Even private health coverage doesn't allocate much for mental health coverage.

The need for community programs that are easily accessible is huge. Support groups, mental health clinics, advocates of mental health that have personal experience – we need all these people working together to create awareness, education and support.

Getting diagnosed for a mental health barrier or disability isn't something that happens in just a one-hour appointment. It's something that takes time and understanding. Especially if you're a parent with a child, take the time to get to understand your child, to read, to talk to other people, to get medical and professional opinions, and to research. Ask your child how they feel. They may not know, but you can help them understand themselves and what they are experiencing.

Society has become reliant on a singular professional's opinion and prescribing medication. Medication isn't bad, but it needs to be monitored and incorporated with other forms of therapy, treatment and self-care. As mentioned in Chapter One, anti-depressant medications have a common side effect of worsening depression or

> *We don't need to be fixed, we are not broken. We just need to learn how to understand and manage, just as a person who breaks a bone needs to rehabilitate it!*

creating suicidal thoughts. Diagnosis is not simple. Mental health is complex, which is a big part of the reason why it's not recognized, understood and often ignored.

Medication is a band-aid and does not cure the condition. It may help temporarily, it might be a stepping-stone for you to get to where you need to be, or can be used to help manage your symptoms; however it does not make them go away. We need to consistently take care of our mental and physical well-being.

There are people with serious or life threatening diagnoses that do really need professional help and medication. For serious conditions, medications can be very helpful but they also need other sources of treatment such as counselling or therapy, family support, program involvement, supervision or the help of a care-aid.

Society

The image of 'normal' society brands is of an airbrushed model on the front cover of a magazine. The image is not even real. Basically, our society is telling us that fake is normal. It tells us we're supposed to look a certain way and the best path to perfect skin and perfectly shaped bodies is of cosmetic surgery, andage defying creams. We are supposed to wear this or wear that, take this magic supplement or pill to achieve normal – when there is no 'normal.'

Who determines these images? It's marketers of multi-trillion dollar companies in the cosmetic industry, the pharmaceutical industry, and the health and fitness industry. Not people that have mental health challenges or people that are in support of people exploring their individuality. These companies make money on branding what people should be and in turn they're actually making people feel bad about themselves.

Society's version of perfect image causes depression, mental health barriers and unhappiness. We need to learn to be happy with ourselves the way that we are and try to do everything we can to make the best of it.

The stigma attached to mental health and disabilities make people with challenges think that they're not good enough and that it is wrong to be like this. Someone going through a divorce or in a wheelchair isn't wrong.

In an effort to reframe the mental health conversation, artist Robot Hugs created a comic, "What if people treated physical illness like mental illness?" Below the images, captions read:

- A man laying in bed and a friend standing beside him saying, "I get that you have food poisoning but you at least have to make an effort"

- A guy with a cut off hand and blood squirting out with a woman saying "you just need to change your frame of mind, then you'll feel better"

- A man getting sick over a toilet and a friend saying "have you tried...you know...not having the flu?"

- A person with diabetes giving themselves an insulin needle and a friend saying "I don't think it's healthy to have to take medication every day just to feel normal. Don't you worry that it's changing you from who you really are?"

If we treated physical health like mental health people would be in fatal condition, yet mental health is just as important and serious and should be taken that way.

We need to ask ourselves if we are actually wanting to change for ourselves rather than someone else or society. If we want to change, we have to take baby steps, make a realistic plan and work at changing. It's not an overnight process. It's something that we have to understand before we can make changes to manage our mental health and disabilities better. I couldn't make changes and manage my mental health and disabilities unless I properly understood them.

> *Ask yourself, "Do I want to change for me, or am I trying to change for someone else or society?"*

If you don't like the way that you look or feel, you have to figure out how to manage it for yourself and no one else. Make sure that you're doing it for you. Ask yourself why looking or acting a certain way makes you unhappy. Is it because of the media or others?

People in your life should love and support you despite what you look or act like, if they don't make you feel that way they are not healthy to have in your life.

How to see past society's perfect image and change our perception:

- Understand that people don't just judge you, if they judge you they are judging everyone
- Realize that the people judging you may be unaware, uninformed or unhappy with themselves
- Remember that society's "image" is photo-shopped and falsified for financial gain
- Learn to relax with what makes you comfortable
- Become more comfortable with who you are
- Enjoy your individuality
- Spend some time with yourself (Yes, just you)
- Remember that people will think what they want to think.
- Worrying is like a rocking chair… Lots of action but going nowhere – remember that
- Try to see the best in others without assuming they see the worst in you
- Occasionally forget about the big picture and focus on the little moments of success and happiness
- Imagine how you will feel once you don't worry as much about what others think
- If you find yourself overthinking, don't think and stew, go do something to take your mind off of it
- Make a list of what you're thankful for
- Smile
- Understand that you are the only person who can cause your negative feelings and that if you feel negative you're allowing someone to trigger that feeling

If you're concerned about your anxiety, weight, acne, anything mental or physical – you need to understand what creates the concern. Do your own research, seek many opinions, professional and not, try solutions, realize and accept that nothing happens overnight. I have really bad acne, I'm 26 years old and I still have adult acne. It makes me self-conscious and angry. I still have really bad anxiety and I dislike it too, but I can manage it. I have learned how to at least have some impact on controlling it.

If someone has a weight problem and diabetes or thyroid issues, they may not actually be able to lose the weight the way that someone without those issues would. They have to properly understand their medical health prior to knowing what diet to go on. Knowing yourself is imperative, knowing what to properly do in order to be healthier and be more fit. Don't listen to society; it's a money grab for health products, cosmetic surgeries and for all of these supplements that you need to take. Just don't listen.

Questions to ask yourself when you are judging yourself;

- Do I want to change for me or am I trying to fit in to society or change for someone else?
- If I change will I actually be happier?
- Will this matter in five years?
- Why is this important to me?
- What support will I have? Where could I find support?
- Will I be happy about my choice or will this process make me even more stressed out?
- Will this benefit my mental health?
- Will this benefit my physical health?
- How much time will this change take? Is it worth it?
- Will this take me away from my job, family, friends, activities, school or other?
- How will this make me better?

I have changed some realistic things in myself such as: managing my anxiety better, improving my reading skills, eating healthier, and exercising. I have also stopped drinking caffeine, learned more about business, practiced meditation and changed my wardrobe to a more professional and mature look. I have also learned how to be a better partner and have more successful relationships.

However, I have also tried to change unrealistic things for others when I was younger, insecure and being bullied: make my Tourette's go away, lose a lot of weight, ignore my family because it wasn't cool, take up sports or activities I really had no interest in, hair color and other physical appearance, adjust my personal taste in food, movies and music and lie about my past or make up stories in high school to fit in.

I understand

I understand what it's like to want to fit in, to get rid of my disabilities and mental health barriers and to just be normal, to want people to not look at me the way that they do or treat me the way that they do. I understand what it's like to have no-one understand you and feel like you're alone every day. I understand what it's like to feel bad and insecure about who you are every day. I also understand what it's like to not take responsibility for anything and to have an excuse for everything.

I understand being embarrassed about it and sheltering myself because of it. I isolated myself for years when I was a victim of my disability and mental health barrier, when it ruled me. I was ashamed to go out in public, I was embarrassed, I distanced myself from my friends, my family and I felt like an outcast from everyone. I'm not here to tell you that you're not doing things well or that you need to change or you won't have a good life. I'm here to tell you that you have unlimited potential to be better and that you can be better.

We can and should feel:

- We're making our own choices for ourselves
- Good about our bodies or like we are on the right path with where we want to be
- We have set out our own values and beliefs
- We can manage our disabilities and mental health
- We have support
- We believe in ourselves or are working on our self-esteem
- Accepting of ourselves, including our flaws that make us who we are
- Under no pressure or stress to change - doing things at our own pace
- It's okay to enjoy being lazy sometimes, physically and mentally
- It's important to enjoy time with our loved ones
- It's okay to enjoy time with ourselves.

How do we overcome worrying what other people think?

This is a difficult thing to do. To some extent I still worry about what other people think, especially business associates and friends. I really care what people think of me – not in a worrisome way – but in that I want to make a positive influence in my relationships and my career. I care about making a good impression with people, I care about letting people know that I am a mental health advocate.

> *"The only limits we have are the limits that we give ourselves!"*
> *– Dr. Wayne Dyer*

Still, I worry when I'm out in public and I have a tic. It's difficult to deal with. I can't stand when people stare at me. It makes me nervous and drives me absolutely bonkers. I worry and I get anxious and I get sweaty.

Overcoming what other people think starts with recognizing that society tells us to be a certain way that's not realistic. Get your head out of magazines, stop looking at advertising, stop buying into health supplements that are going to be a magical weight loss pill or magically make you look better. On whose judgment do you need to look better?

After Photoshop   Before Photoshop

Most media images of the perfect person are modified for advertising. Knowing that will help you stop worrying about what other people think. When you gain more understanding about yourself and define more of yourself, you'll be more confident and you'll eventually not worry about it. Gaining that confidence is key.

But first you need to understand yourself and your mental health and disabilities before you can define yourself and before you can be more confident. Learn to love yourself with these things. Worrying about this never goes away 100%, but that's all part of being a human being – everybody worries about it, even the most confident people in the world. I know I certainly still do.

I worry about making the best impression with my career and being successful in business. I worry about my health when I eat too many sweets, when people stare at me when I have a tic, that my partner will one day not be able to handle my anxiety, that things won't work out the way that I plan, that my chronic pain will never go away or I will never recover. I also worry about small things that are really pointless. I never give up and do my best to not let it get to me, but I have to move on to something positive and happy in order to not let worry get to me. It's normal to worry, but years ago I realized that it's actually quite pointless. I have turned my worry around to something positive; if I didn't worry about things, I wouldn't have nearly the drive and ambition that I do. Worrying and overthinking actually causes me to push myself further. What's not great about that?!

You are extraordinary just the way that you are now. Surround yourself with people who also struggle with this. A support group can help by giving you an opportunity to talk to people who feel the same. Know that you're not alone. Spread the awareness to stop the stigma!

How do we start influencing people to see images other than what society brands?

Be confident in yourself. When people can see you're confident about your mental health barriers and disabilities, it rubs off on others, giving them a different perspective, which leads to hope and inspiration.

> *Speak of yourself proudly, others tend to feel the same way about you as you feel about yourself!*

I mentioned in Chapter Two that 2016 was the sixth TeleMiracle that I have volunteered at and been involved with. People are often always looking at me weird with my tics. There are literally thousands of volunteers at TeleMiracle who I knew would be noticing my tics. This year my goal was to educate people about my Tourette's and be extremely transparent, light hearted and honest about it. I wore the Tourette's shirt that I made, it says "I have Tourette's Syndrome – It's not easy to live with!"

Throughout the night, volunteers and people in the audience were stopping me so they could read my shirt. 95% of the people that read my shirt said, "Oh, ha ha, that's funny!" I would respond in a very calm manner with a little sense of humour and say "No, I actually have Tourette's." They would say, "No you don't!" I would respond (*again with a good sense of humour*), "Mmmm, yep I'm pretty sure that I do…"

I was usually met by silence. They were either embarrassed or confused. Most people assume that Tourette's behaviour is yelling vulgar words like they show in the movies. That's actually not true. That's called *Coprolalia* and it only occurs in 7% of people with Tourette's.

Many were surprised by this. I told them what my symptoms are. (*I usually had some sort of tic when I was speaking with them and would point it out as Tourette's.*) They told me that they would have never guessed that. I would reply, "I get that a lot – don't worry about it."

As I walked away, most of them turned towards someone else and say, "She actually has Tourette's and it's not always swearing" in a respectfully educated way. I even heard "That girl's actually got Tourette's, cool!"

I of course, loved that one and I walked away saying to myself, "Yeah, it's cool!" I have never felt so good about my Tourette's. People listened, wanted to be educated and asked questions out of genuine curiosity rather than judging. I welcomed them to ask any questions and told them that I was completely comfortable and would be honest. One of my fellow Kinette's walked up to me and said, "Do you mind if I ask you a question? It's kind of personal and you don't have to answer. I don't mean anything bad by it." I welcomed it and she asked me if my tics get worse when I'm tired and stressed (*by this time I had been up for almost 24 hours*). I told her without hesitation that it did and she could ask me any other questions she wanted, not to be embarrassed. She smiled and walked away.

When I'm not wearing a shirt, I tell anyone that stares, looks curious or even judgemental that I have Tourette's Syndrome and it's not easy to live with. People instantly change their vibes towards me and go from the fallback of judging to understanding, curious and caring. They often feel bad that they have judged too. Educate others. They don't know – and you don't know how they will respond until you do!

Help boost other people's confidence. It gives you a confidence boost when you can make somebody else feel good about their own situation. Voice your own opinion and feelings and don't be ashamed. Speak proudly, voicing your thoughts and beliefs loudly. Paying this forward is huge! Even if you're having a rough day, making people feel better about themselves, helping them and giving that support makes you feel better. It might actually turn around your day! When I make someone else feel good or believe in themselves, the feeling is irreplaceable. Seeing your message make a difference in peoples lives is truly what I live for!

What can you say to others to see past society's image?

1. Remind them:
- They are not alone
- Society's version of image is false
- They are unique and genuine

2. Tell them a story to relate to

3. Invite them to a support group or forward them to another resource.

5

Understanding Your
Mental Health and Disability

I didn't understand my mental health and disabilities until I was 20 years old. When I was 17 I tried to figure it out, but only in the hopes of making my Tourette's go away so I could say that I no longer had Tourette's. I knew that a person could grow out of Tourette's by their late teens to early adulthood and I was hoping that I would be in that 30%.

I went to my first psychiatrist with my parents when I was six. I went for the first time on my own when I was 17. I hoped that he would tell me that I no longer have Tourette's. He confirmed that not only did I still have Tourette's and ADHD, I also had OCD, anxiety and panic disorder. This was not good news.

The psychiatrist gave me a prescription for OCD and I was on that for six months. It did not help, so I went off. After spending so much time trying to figure out how to get rid of my Tourette's, and now knowing that I never could made me realize I just had to accept it. The hardest part was admitting that I was a victim. Once I started to come to terms with that fact, I started to turn my life around. I'm still learning and understanding my disabilities and how they affect me. They have drastically changed my life for better and worse.

Your mental health and disability is a part of who you are. Learn to be proud of it, embrace it and use it to your advantage. Our mental health barriers and disabilities are what make us who we are just as any other person's barriers are. If you learn how to channel it properly, it can make a world of a difference to your life. There are many different ways of understanding your disability and learning to manage it well. Having a mental health barrier or disability makes you an exceptional individual and it's really a gift. You just need to find the right tools to use it as a strength; with any weakness or challenge that we have there is always a way to find the positivity and the right path. When life throws us obstacles, if we search for the best parts about the worst things, something good can come out of every situation. Life challenges and continues to test us, it's the universe's way of making us stronger individuals. It's about perception and how we reflect on our life and perceive the events that are happening to us. Those obstacles and our choices in how to handle them define who we are, whether positive or negative, secure or insecure, happy or unhappy.

> *Your mental health and disability is a part of who you are, that's a really great thing!*

Mental health and disability issues have been recently raised more in our society, but it's not close to where it needs to be. Being aware of others' mental health can make a large impact in others' invisible lives, positive or negative. Understanding your own mental health and disabilities is crucial, however, it's almost more important to recognize and be aware of others. We all need to start being aware of ourselves and others that may be struggling with these challenges. We should be working together aggressively to create more awareness. Stop the stigma! Stop the bullying! Helping others by working together in support of each other rather than against or judging each other. In our society, most people simply don't understand mental health and disabilities. They don't judge just to judge, they judge because they don't understand. Judging is a fallback for the unknown, people fear the unknown.

To build my understanding of my mental health and disabilities, I:

- Did research on the internet (from credible and medical sources)
- Read books (if you don't like reading at the time so instead I listened to audio books)
- Read articles (magazines, on social media and through associations for mental health)
- Got medical input (doctors, psychiatrists, psychologists, naturopaths, relaxation therapists, pharmacists)
- Asked for advice from family and peers (who also deal with mental health barriers and disabilities)
- Forced myself to have time alone (this may be difficult at first)
- Went to a support group.

I was fortunate having someone close to me that also suffers. My dad has been living with ADHD and anxiety most – and has been very understanding, helpful and supportive, which made things easier for me.

In your search, you're going to find discouraging things and uplifting things, things that you can relate to you and things that you just can't. Don't rely on one piece of information or one person's advice on understanding yourself. Take everything into account that you read or hear. Mental health and disabilities are different for everyone.

It's often overwhelming because there will be many things that you learn about yourself, and taking the time to get to learn how your disability and mental health barrier affects you is important. You will be pleasantly surprised to find out who you really are with your barriers. Look forward to your self-discovery and self-definition.

How can we understand our mental health or understand the mental health of someone close to us? Use this time to:

- Educate yourself – research on-line, read books, speak with certified professionals and people who experience mental health challenges for themselves

- Learn the signs, symptoms and effects, mental health and disabilities can affect people in many ways and in all areas of life

- Reach out to associations – Mental Health Associations, Anxiety Association, Learning Disabilities Association for advice and support

- Take a mental health first aid course

- Learn to be self-aware, document your thinking and awareness, keep a journal, ask someone close to you to pay attention and mention it to you – If you don't like writing, use your computer or phone to make notes, take some pictures and log an album in your phone

- If you are not sure how to be aware, ask someone close to you to pay attention and have a discussion about how they can bring it up to you in a constructive way that you're both comfortable with

- Have realistic expectations – don't expect to cure yourself or make things better overnight

- Realize the feelings of loneliness, shame and guilt are normal

- Don't get overwhelmed - stay calm while learning and getting to know your mental health

- Understand that mental illness and disabilities affect not just the individual but the people surrounding them as well

- Understand that mental health barriers and disabilities are normal and 1 in 4 people will experience mental illness at some point in their life
- Lastly, make new friends that can relate to you and that you can comfortably talk to. If you don't know how to find friends like this, reach out to an association. Associations have really great resources for connecting people and may also have a support group where you won't feel judged.

Nurture your mental health, give yourself the tender loving care that you need, give yourself the time because you're worth it. Don't just go sit down with psychiatrists for an hour and get a diagnosis. Yes, they can give you somewhere to start, but don't stop after that one appointment.

Each and every person is different. If twenty people have anxiety and diagnosed ADHD, each one of those twenty people's anxiety and ADHD limits and affects them differently. My anxiety is not quite like what another's is and vice versa. Some people have social anxiety and some generalized anxiety. An individual's ADHD may cause them to struggle in school with general motivation or focus. Understanding

Each and every person is unique and you need to find out what works for you!

your mental health challenge is not a textbook formula, a written formula or a psychiatric formula, it's a specific sequence that works for you and something that you have to figure out for yourself. If you don't take the time to get there, you're never going to move forward and break your barriers.

I found out that each area was affected a little bit differently and some better than others, some weren't affected. Trial and error was my best friend, I tried some silly and complex things. Some made it worse for me and overwhelmed. Keep trying and don't give up.

What can you start doing to help yourself?

- The most important place to start is to practice mindfulness (relaxing and quieting your thoughts and mind). As a person with anxiety and panic disorder I know how difficult this may be, but try activities like yoga, meditation, or going for a walk.

- Value yourself (treat yourself with self-respect, kindness and less criticism)

- Take care of your body (nutritional meals, lots of water and exercise)

- Limit cigarettes, caffeine, drugs and alcohol

- Surround yourself with supportive and loving people, and get rid of the poison ones

- Practice positive stress management techniques

- Try something new (an activity or food).

- Give your time (volunteer for a cause you believe in or an activity that you like). Helping others and being selfless is rejuvenating.

- Set realistic goals and don't set yourself up for failure - achieving smaller goals continuously is better than not achieving large goals.

Relationships and your mental health and disabilities

Family, friends, life partners and co-workers affect your mental health and disabilities and vice versa. Without proper communication, awareness and effort, it can be a very negative and confusing thing in your relationships. It can cause unnecessary break-ups, fights and conflicts. In my previous relationships, it caused a large amount of problems.

Problems that this can cause in relationships; (From either party)

- Extreme frustration
- Contempt
- Unloving feelings
- Fights (verbal and physical)
- Abuse (verbal and physical)
- Unhappiness
- Guilt
- Self-esteem issues
- Trust issues.

Relationships are built on trust and communication so you should communicate about your disability and mental health barrier in a light and comfortable mood. In order to do this you need to understand your own mental health and disabilities, as I focused on earlier in this chapter.

People that you have relationships with need to understand and be supportive, and they often want to be. However, we can't expect them to be if we're not being open, upfront and educating them about our challenges. We should be providing them all the information and understanding that we can so they can give the best support.

People can't help without understanding. They want to help, but it's our job to help them understand!

Supportive relationships can help you be the best person that you can, give you strength, or ensure someone is there in times of weakness. This support system can be established when you communicate your challenges clearly and have an open discussion without eliminating details that may be embarrassing. Don't hold back those details. People that truly care for you won't judge you, instead they will want to help. Be completely open and transparent in your discussions. People want to help you, people have great hearts within our society and they judge not because they want to be judgemental but because they don't understand. If you ask somebody for help or support they want to do that but most people don't know how to be supportive until they understand – so they have a fallback of judging. I get judged all of the time for my motor tics with Tourette's, but as soon as I educate them and help them understand, everything is different. Their entire vibe and behaviour is different towards me. If you don't understand your own self, you can't get anyone else to. You're going to struggle throughout relationships.

One day, I was in the bank waiting in line. I had pretty high anxiety that day so of course my tics were bad. An older woman near the teller looked back at me with a disgusted look. I am used to weird looks thanks to my Tourette's, so I thought nothing of it. She continued to look back at me multiple times. Finally, I thought that this was my opportunity to educate her. I waited for the next time she would look back at me and said in a quiet voice, "Hello, I have Tourette's Syndrome and it's not easy to live with." She didn't say a word but the look on her face changed instantly from judgement to guilt and embarrassment. She became ashamed, put her head down as she walked out of the bank without making eye contact with anyone. It was not my intent to embarrass her and, to be honest, I actually felt bad afterwards. I did however manage to educate her and make her aware of my situation and know that from now on she will think twice before judging someone's situation. This is a perfect example of somebody just being unaware or uneducated about mental health and disabilities – a completely harmless and honest woman.

How can you receive better support and understanding from your partner if you're struggling?

- Understand your own challenges and communicate them
- Once you understand, tell your partner what you need for support
- Don't shy away from them or be embarrassed (the less you judge yourself, the less others judge you)
- Be comfortable in your own shoes and don't feel belittled or lesser in your relationship, we are all equal
- Take time for yourself to think about what you need and how to ask for it
- Let yourself be vulnerable and let your partner in, trust them
- Join a support group and bring your partner with you
- Ask for support
- Seek individual help for yourself
- Talk about it! (BIG ONE)
- Have fun and enjoy your relationship. Every relationship (intimate, family, professional or other) has its challenges that need to be worked through and some are completely unrelated to mental health or disabilities.

How can you be supportive to your partner?

- Accept their feelings, reassure them that they are not alone
- Join a support group for spouses
- Educate yourself, research, sign up to educational forums, read books
- Ask if they need help or what they need

- Ask questions about it
- Encourage them to do small things or activities
- Be open minded
- Talk about it and encourage them to talk about it
- Encourage them to come up with coping and stress management strategies or do it together
- Just be there, even if you don't know what to say

How can our school, work and activities be affected by mental health barriers and disabilities?

They can cause:
- Embarrassment
- Negativity
- Self doubt
- Absenteeism
- Poor performance
- Stress
- Poor academic grades
- Procrastination
- Feeling unwell, calling in sick
- Not being able to focus
- Getting easily overwhelmed
- Feeling lack of intelligence
- Poor social skills

Unlike when I was in school and my early days of work, things are a lot different. Now there's more school and employer awareness with educators and employers introducing programs that focus on mental health and disabilities.

Throughout my school years, I thought that I was stupid because I didn't do well and received many failing marks. Even when I felt that I tried my hardest. I was forced to take pages of notes that I would never remember as my peers, to read the same books, write tests in the same time period, to write essays and follow text books. All I needed was to learn a different way, but the resources weren't available for me to ask for in the educational system.

My parents, teachers and employers just didn't understand and even if they tried to understand they didn't know what to do about it. Teachers, employers, co-workers, associates in your school, work and activities need to understand just as much as the people that you have personal relationships with. They're there to help but they're not mind readers so you have to communicate and let them know how you need help. You need to ask for the help that you need.

If you need to do things in a different way so you can succeed, you need to know that and know what to ask for. This means that you need to know what areas or tasks are your strengths and what areas or tasks you need help with. There are many options today for assisting people with mental health barriers and disabilities; programs, electronic tools and software, tutors, special accommodations,

I felt like I was stupid and hopeless when it turned out I was very bright and just needed to learn in a different way!

financial assistance or coverage for mental health care. These all encourage people to get an education, and a good job and to be involved in activities – regardless of whether they have a mental health barrier or disability or not. All we need to do is ask for help and not to be ashamed of doing that. Be upfront with people, they want to help you. Take the time to figure out what you need because if you don't it's hard for others to help and be supportive.

Here's some ways that I learn best;

- Hands-on (I always loved mechanics and shop in school, they were my highest grades)

- Putting things I read into my own words (I do not have a strong spoken vocabulary)

- Linking things - relating it to something else in a way that I can see or understand. (For a simple example, remembering a grocery list like Milk, Honey and Apples. Imagine a giant cow that had bees that came from its udders instead of milk. For the honey and apples, imagine bees pollinating apple seeds or a honeycomb made out of an apple. This sounds silly but amazing how well it works when you can visualize.)

- Pretend I'm trying to explain it to a first grader (simplify it as much as possible leaving you less overwhelmed)

- Try to enjoy learning (make a comfortable environment with things like: tea, music, warm blanket (but not too warm so you fall asleep), comfortable chair , a pet on your lap or lots of light)

- Asked someone close to me to work through it with me

- Diagrams (draw it out or have someone draw out what they're trying to explain)

- Use your finger when you read to follow along and not get lost in the context (this makes my reading faster and easier)

- Give yourself a break. (When I am working on something I give myself a 10-minute break every 20 minutes. If I do not do this, I get overwhelmed and have a hard time staying attentive)

Why is it important to understand?

Firstly, you can't overcome what you don't understand so others can't be supportive if they don't understand. People are not mind readers and a high percentage of the population has not been educated on mental health and disabilities. They're basically starting from scratch when they get to know you. Assume that they know nothing about mental health or disabilities and it's your job to educate them so you can have the best possible relationship.

Secondly, you can't learn how to channel your mental health barriers and disabilities to use them as a strength if you don't understand yourself. You can't ask for help if you don't know what kind of help you need and you can't try to overcome, improve and get better if you don't understand what you need. When you understand you, with your

> *You can't learn how to positively channel your disabilities and mental health to use as a strength if you don't understand yourself!*

mental health barriers and disabilities, you can have better relationships. Your work, school and activities will be better, happier and stronger.

Taking the time and patience to understand

This is very important and doesn't happen overnight and is a slow and frustrating process.

What do we get frustrated about?

- The "Should," – "I should have gotten that done, should have this more money, should look much better, should be better off than I am, should not be where I am, not be who I am or be someone else." These statements make you feel guilty for where you are.

- Not seeing instant results

- Anxiety

- Lack of proper support or people that care about me. (Get rid of poisonous people, there are always support groups and other supportive resources you just have to look for them)

- Feeling I'm not good enough, and don't I deserve this, or I can't do this. (Because YOU CAN! That's it, plain and simple)

We discuss about how to overcome these frustrations in Chapter 6. Once you recognize and admit to yourself that you're holding yourself back, making your own life's course, and not buying into society telling you that you can't do things – you've got your first step done! After that, time is the most important and crucial factor. You need to get to know yourself with your mental health and disabilities and stop trying to be who you're not without them. Understanding and knowing what you need is an ongoing process and will always be changing. This is why being self-aware and understanding is so important. I figure out something new every day about myself, or about how to manage something better than I did. I figure out different tricks and tactics through reading. My ongoing goal is to educate myself even after 20 years of having my diagnoses.

When I first started understanding, I didn't know what I needed, so trying to explain it to people was next to impossible. Initially I started explaining to people what I did understand, which wasn't much but getting the ball rolling with talking about it was a great start. This also gave me clarification on my own understanding by just talking about it. Talking things through with people that you love and who care about you often results in a really great solution, or at the very least relief in getting the issue off your chest.

I got so overwhelmed and frustrated, it felt like I was never going to get better. I had major anxiety, but that's a very normal part of this process, especially if you already have anxiety. Don't let it get to you! At one point, I had over 300 lists in the note organizing software, Evernote, and I didn't even know how the items all got there. I got so overwhelmed with how many lists that I had, I quit for a while and I had to restart. I spent so much time organizing how to be organized, my head was spinning. Trying to analyze the information that you get can be very difficult and overwhelming. You may be a little lost on how to handle it at first, but trust me you'll get the hang of it. Sometimes, I will read a business article or mental health article that's great information, but too much to

> *Tomorrow is another day*
>
> *Today was better than yesterday*
>
> *Everyone has bad days and it's okay to have a bad day*
>
> *Frustration and impatience make your productivity and effectiveness worse*

take in at once for me. I often ask myself how am I going to deal with this information and implement these ideas – and even that's too much to comprehend sometimes with my anxiety. If your thoughts get overwhelming during this process, let them sit for an hour or a day. Sleep on it. Wake up the next morning and revisit it.

How can you be patient and believe in yourself?

- Take slow and deep breaths
- Break your anxiety cycle - change what you're doing when you have anxiety or get frustrated
- Learn to manage your emotions and stress
- Have a relaxing activity
- Force yourself to relax physically and slow down (Kindly remind yourself and relax each muscle from your head to your toes telling yourself each muscle as you relax them)
- Support yourself with positive people
- Positive self-talk
- Gratitude journal
- Make a success scrap book and put small things in it to start like making the bed, doing the dishes or going for a walk
- Acknowledge and accept your negative self-talk, but don't allow it to affect you
- Trust yourself and your decisions.

Things work out a lot better for me when I'm not overwhelmed. I can process things after they've resonated with me for a while. I still get anxiety every day, but once I take that time, the result is life changing. Mental health *(positive or negative)* becomes a part of your habits, built into your mind and just part of normal day-to-day living. Anxiety is a part of who I am, it's also a big part of what makes me successful. I have found how to channel my anxiety in a positive manner to make me more successful and you can do that too with your mental health barriers and disabilities. People call them mental health illnesses. I completely disagree with the word illness. Even if something is chemically wrong within your body or your brain – with the right support, medical and natural help and the right belief in yourself, it can be managed! We all have unlimited potential! I believe that a lot of mental illness is called an illness or is able to become an illness because there's not early enough recognition and, once they realize it's an illness, it's much more difficult to manage. That's what I'm here for, working towards awareness and understanding, educating people so mental health illness doesn't have to be so severe.

After I lost one of my very close friends in 2011 to suicide from schizoaffective disorder, his family and I looked back on his death and we said that we wished we could have been closer to him. He pulled away from even the closest people in his life. Of course at the time we never thought that it would have led to what it did.

> *Giving up is the only true failure!*

His parents shared some of his challenges with me. He claimed that if people understood him better, especially the doctors, he would have been able to conquer the illness and he felt that he would have been able to believe in himself more. If he could just feel, he said. The medication that he was on caused him not to feel anything, good or bad. I can't even begin to imagine what that would be like to not feel.

It's very frustrating when people don't understand what you're going through. I've been there myself, where I've felt like nobody was really there. I felt like I couldn't talk to anyone. No one understood me. I was alone in the world. These thoughts are why mental illness becomes an illness.

You are not alone. Mental illness can be aided and sometimes prevented with the right support, awareness and education.

6

Who You Are and Want To Be

In other chapters, I explain the importance of understanding your mental health and disabilities. Being self-aware is crucial to overcome your mental health and disability challenges. Without building that understanding, you will always experience challenges in your relationships, at school, at work and in activities.

It may be an overwhelming and frustrating process. You may feel like you're not making any progress. But change doesn't happen overnight, don't forget to be patient.

Take the time to get to know yourself

You deserve your own time just as much as anyone else. I have 'me' time in some very silly ways but they work for me. I continue to do them regardless of how small the task (*if anybody else saw me do them they would think I was going bonkers*).

> *Be patient with yourself.*

I do things like:

- Talk to myself in the mirror
- Sing to myself
- Dance with my broom around the house
- Go to movies at the theatre alone
- Go for a drive
- Have bubble baths
- Colour
- Watch cartoons (Oh yeah - They bring me back to my childhood for comfort)
- Listen to music from the late 90s (It picks me up)
- Go for walks and sometimes skip
- Play and talk with my pets (dog and horses - they don't talk back…)

You will end up discovering yourself, and enjoy being the person that you are. You will be pleasantly surprised by how many things you end up loving about yourself. You will end up loving alone time. Outside of my relationship and business I spend 99% of my time alone. I love every minute of it.

Continuing to have 'me' time is important to maintain your self-awareness; when you recognize things quickly, they can be corrected as soon as you see them. I also love spending as much time as I can with my partner because he embraces the person that I am with my mental health and disabilities. He feels that it's a part of me, and loves me for it. Having that support from him is amazing, he is my rock. I often feel more embarrassed than he does about my tics and anxious habits – he doesn't even notice them anymore.

Everyone deserves their own time!

70

If none of these appeal to you, here's some things you could try;

- Listening to music
- Scrapbook or crafts
- Write out your values and goals
- Ask yourself what your personality is and really think about it
- Get to know your body, take care of it with proper nutrition and exercise
- Read
- Allow yourself to dream as if nothing is impossible
- Be honest about your likes and dislikes
- Study your strengths and weaknesses
- Give yourself credit for small achievements
- Find three small things that you like about yourself and work on a growing list from there.

Define who you are

Your mental health and disabilities are a huge part of what made you the person that you are today, but you are not your mental health barrier or disability. It does not rule you, you rule it! It is a part of who you are and you have the choice of how it affects you positively or negatively. Most importantly, it makes you an exceptional individual, so find your strengths in it and how it has benefited you. I'm sure that we can all look back and find a way that it has benefited us, even if we have to dig really deep.

I discussed earlier in the book how we often forget to give ourselves credit where credit is due, how we overlook the small little things we achieve because we're always thinking that we're never doing good quite enough. If you add up the small achievements throughout the course of your life – it ends up being a pretty big thing to be credited for. Maybe your mental health and disabilities make you more organized, more hands-on or visual, more passionate about organizations or a specific field of work. You have a huge heart, and use what you have been given as a gift.

> *Be who you are with your disabilities and mental health barriers, do not try to be without them!*

Define who you want to be

It's really important that you don't try to change who you are. This means defining who you want to be with your mental health and disabilities. Sit down and write out your values and deep beliefs. Stick to those beliefs and values to avoid being compromised. Set boundaries with people in your life and the new people that you meet.

My values are;

- Being honest and respectful of people

- Smiling, laughing and being silly

- Helping others

- Being the best person that I can be every day

- Following my life dreams and aspirations

- Being positive and optimistic

- Being a part of a good support group

- Being kind and caring of others, including removing myself from those surroundings that I'm uncomfortable with

It's helpful to set those boundaries when you first meet people. You have to let them know what you're comfortable with and others should be respectful of that.

Find Role Models who you admire as a person

This could be an actor, musician, mentor, family member, co-worker, boss, business owner or author. Choose specific traits of those people that are important to you to have like confidence, business sense, humour, organizational skills, reliability, intelligence or energy. Realize that you are capable of being anyone that you want to be and need to quit living in the dark, being embarrassed and unhappy with who you are because society tells you that you're not normal and you're different.

Once you know what traits are important to you, establish what kind of person you want to be without compromising who you are. You can always better yourself, become more confident, expand your knowledge, increase your business sense, be more organized but don't compromise who you are with your passions, values and deep beliefs because of someone or something else. Find people that will be supporting you, while respecting your moral values and deep beliefs.

Every person in this world has been unsure of themselves, the people that succeed are the ones that spend the time to figure out who they are, define who they want to be and never give up on themselves. Everybody that succeeds has failed tons of times and the people that succeed are simply the ones that don't give up. They're not particularly lucky or have it easy or just had things handed to them, they're people that constantly are working towards their goals and all you see is the face value of their success. Look how many times these people failed.

How many times others tried before they succeeded!

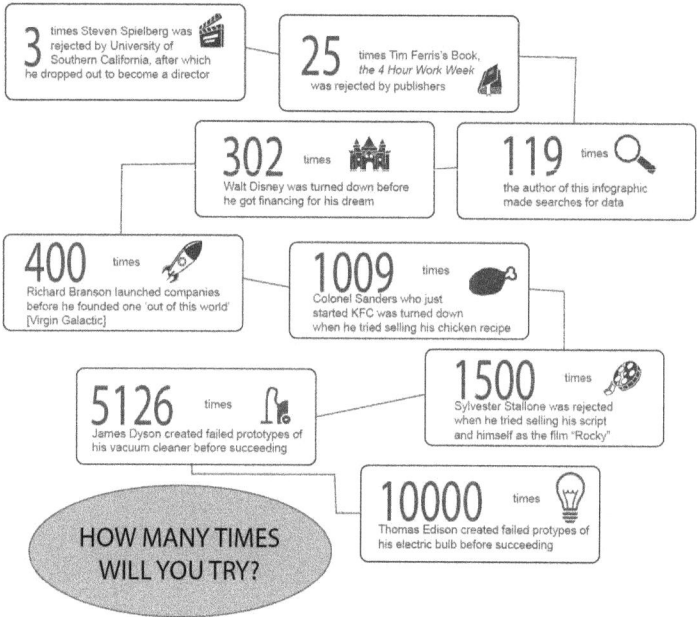

3 times Steven Spielberg was rejected by University of Southern California, after which he dropped out to become a director

25 times Tim Ferris's Book, *the 4 Hour Work Week* was rejected by publishers

302 times
Walt Disney was turned down before he got financing for his dream

119 times
the author of this infographic made searches for data

400 times
Richard Branson launched companies before he founded one 'out of this world' [Virgin Galactic]

1009 times
Colonel Sanders who just started KFC was turned down when he tried selling his chicken recipe

1500 times
Sylvester Stallone was rejected when he tried selling his script and himself as the film "Rocky"

5126 times
James Dyson created failed prototypes of his vacuum cleaner before succeeding

10000 times
Thomas Edison created failed protypes of his electric bulb before succeeding

HOW MANY TIMES WILL YOU TRY?

Graphic by Rod Francis

You will always grow as an individual

Even once you have become the person that you sought to be, there will be more ways to grow. There will never be a point where you can't grow or achieve something greater or be somebody better. Continuing to grow as an individual is exciting, it feels great to know and be proud of who you are. I love expanding who I am, learning more about myself, discovering how else I can be a better person, partner, speaker or business woman. Life is overwhelming at times, but I love the process and constantly surprise myself with what I discover about myself.

Once I actually try things that I never thought I would try or do, I surprise myself. I would never have had that experience if I held back out of fear or rejection. When I was younger, I never had the slightest thought to be an author. I didn't like reading or writing mainly because I wasn't good at either. The feeling of achievement is irreplaceable when became an author. I proved to myself that I can do anything, including being an author with ADHD and a learning disability.

There comes a point where you look back on your life, who you were and how much you have grown and it all seemed so easy even thought the journey is really the opposite. I look back on my life now and wonder how I got to where I am. The answer that I have for myself is persistence and perseverance. I pushed through when I didn't think that I could or didn't believe in myself. I figured if all

Always strive to be a better person and help others!

these other people can fail so many times and still have success, I should at least have a crack at it right? There's got to be some small chance that I could, and eventually the trying started paying off and getting easier. I didn't fail any less, the failure just got easier. I started to believe in myself and be happy with my life. A big thing that kept me going is that I was helping others; making other people happy made me happy. Knowing that I could help others meant the world to me and I gained hope out of that knowledge. It's an amazing feeling when you can know at the end of the day that you changed somebody's day.

7

The Three Approaches

I have three approaches to learning how to use your mental health challenges and disabilities as a strength.

The First Approach → Accept it.

Accept what you cannot change and change what you cannot accept. You're you, learn to be okay with that and eventually learn to be proud of that. You're different and you're not the only one, being different is a gift.

Being different makes you unique. Each and every person has their different challenges and having a mental health challenge and disability is just one of those challenges. Some people have physical disabilities, academic

DID YOU KNOW?

Individuals with mental health challenges and disabilities often have extremely high IQ's and most of the world's geniuses struggled with mental health? (Albert Einstein, Abraham Lincoln, Beethoven, Edvard Munch, Michelangelo, Charles Dickens, Isaac Newton)

challenges, relationship challenges, insecurities, past traumatic situations, medical conditions or career challenges. Those challenges are no better or worse than ours. We are all equal.

Steps to 'Accept It';

- Realize you're not broken and you don't need to be fixed

- Realize it's not your fault

- Don't overthink it and just let it be

- Get to know you for you (not who others or society want you to be)

- Be honest with yourself

- Realize that society's version of "normal" is not real

- Understand that most people have challenges: mental, physical or emotional

- Find a good support system or use one you already have

- Read inspiring stories that may be similar to yours and look for others that can inspire you

- Allow yourself to be not okay (not being okay IS okay - don't fight what you're feeling and acknowledge that the feeling is there and be okay with it)

- Do things that make you feel good about yourself

- Realize that it's okay to need help and have moments of weakness

- Forgive yourself

Don't compare yourself to others or don't judge yourself for your weaknesses, mental health or disabilities. We don't have to allow them to be weaknesses and disabling. Your mental health and disability is a part of you, and that's a really great thing. Having a mental health challenge or disability makes you an exceptional individual. It's really a gift, you just need to find the right tools to use them as a strength and in a positive manner.

The Second Approach → Change your feelings and perspective.

If I change my feelings and perspective, I begin to see my struggles and mistakes differently. If I deal with the task at hand rather than focusing on the result and am specific when correcting and dealing with situations I feel differently about myself. For example, I need to say, "I messed that up," rather than, "I'm messed up."

Give yourself credit when you complete a task or do well – even the small little things. You made the bed this morning → credit. You took the dog for a walk → credit. You had a salad instead of a burger → credit. You finished a task at work on time → credit. Don't dwell on the things that you didn't get done, give yourself credit for the other ones that you *did* do which starts a positive chain reaction.

I talk about the positivity and optimism ripple effect in earlier chapters. When you feel good about completing one thing, you'll have more motivation and ambition to complete others, your success provokes more of the same!

Steps to changing your feelings and perspective:

Know:

- You are worthy of love
- You are enough
- You are strong
- How to be self-compassionate
- How your mental health and disabilities define you positively
- To give yourself credit for small achievements

Do:
- Ask for help
- Take care of your mind and body
- Meditate
- Listen to music
- Yoga or exercise
- Deal with one thing at a time

One of my good friends has depression and said to me, "I hate being depressed, being depressed is bad."

My response was, "Who says that it's not okay and bad?"

She responded, "Well it's just not accepted and it's bad."

I said, "Okay well then if no-one important to you specifically is saying it's bad then, why are you letting it impact how you feel about it?"

She didn't know. I asked how her depression defines her in a positive way and what good personality traits it brings her. She paused for quite sometime and at first said nothing so I asked her to really think about it.

She responded, "Well, it makes me really care about others and be aware of how they're feeling."

I encouraged her to go on and within ten minutes she came up with the following in addition: it makes her good at her job of being a paramedic, it allows her to be very analytical and creative, she can show her partner unconditional love and accept his, she is close with her family, she is very aware of her feelings and can process her emotions. By the end of our conversation, she felt uplifted and allowed herself to embrace her depression. By the time she hung up the phone I could hear confidence in her voice. Her feelings had turned completely around.

The Third Approach → Transform.

Learn to be proud of you for you. Just be you, and change what you can't accept and can be changed. You can't change your mental health or your disabilities, but you can change how they affect you and your life. Let your attitude about your weaknesses, differences, mental health or disabilities define you in a positive way.

Avoid trying to fit into society and what we're told should be normal. There is no normal. We're just as normal as a person that is going through a divorce, struggling to find a job, having a mid-life crisis, having financial struggles or having a physical disability.

Having a mental health challenge or disability is a gift. It's the universe's way of making us amazing and unique individuals. It's there to make you genuine. I love my OCD and anxiety. Without them I would not have the organizational skills that I have, or be a businessperson or an author. I probably wouldn't have even started a business. Without my ADHD, I wouldn't be able to speak in front of a crowd or to host and produce a TV and radio show. Without my anxiety, OCD, Tourette's syndrome and ADHD, I wouldn't be the person that I am today – talking about this with the level of experience and inspiration that I have.

> *I love my mental health and disabilities! Find what you love about yours.*

Find somebody who may not fully understand or experience it themselves, but tries to be there and understand. You have to surround yourself with a positive group of people. The people that you associate with and are in relationships with can be leeches and draining – or they can be pushers and motivators. My partner pushes me and motivates me. If I ever say I can't do something, he calls me out and then asks me how I am going to do it. That influence makes all of the difference in the world.

If you don't have somebody at home or you're alone, or if you have a negative support system – you need to do something to turn that around. Join a support group. Get some positive guidance.

Find somebody uplifting, or go to a Mental Health Association branch. Just find people that can motivate you, push you forward and pull you up when you're struggling.

Steps to transform the way you feel:

- Practice healthy habits
- Speak up and educate people about mental health and disabilities
- Determine how this defines you in a positive way
- Give yourself lenience for the weaknesses
- Set realistic goals for yourself
- Do work and activities that give you purpose
- Surround yourself with positive influences
- Get rid of poisonous people in your life
- Know you're in good company with yourself
- Let your pain and/or suffering fuel you and become your positive power
- Do nice things for yourself

So you've got Tourette's? Awesome!

How about anxiety? Great!

Have depression? Cool!

What about ADHD? Sweet!

(All about your perspective)

Why are these important steps?

You have to learn how to accept yourself and your mental health barrier and disability. Without this you can't make progress and you can't grow your full potential. If you don't accept it and are always trying to fight it, you're never going to progress. It's important not to waste energy thinking negatively about it, yet I see many people spending energy trying to change what they can't and dwelling on what they have no control over. They feel sorry for themselves, blaming everything on something or someone else. If those people spent just 10% of the time towards something positive that they spend being negative, or complaining about how unhappy and out of control of the situation they are, they'd be moving ahead more than they think is possible. 10% of the negative energy that people waste on thoughts and actions that are never going to go anywhere for them could tip the scales for them if they used that energy in a positive way.

Once you start transforming the way that you think and feel about things, you'll be surprised how much effect the small things actually have. If you're ashamed or embarrassed, it brings you down and that energy rubs off onto others and does the same for them. If you're proud of it, speak proudly and informatively and be open with people about it. When you're comfortable in your own shoes, other people are much more accepting of you. But if you're uneasy, people can feel that and pick up on it. That will have a negative ripple effect back to you which is stressful. You will always have doubts. Unfortunately, those will never go away. I still have doubts every day, but now I have a lot of techniques and tools that work for me.

What you give your attention to you will receive back, whether it's positive or negative. I believe in the universe's power of energy called *The Law of Attraction* as described by Esther and Jerry Hicks. If you're putting out positive energy, you're going to get that back. If you're putting out negative energy, you're going to get that back also. Have you ever had road rage, been frustrated and in a rush?

You're upset or angry. You hit all of the red lights or the only train you've had to wait for in months! Did you notice how on those times the traffic seems to get worse or you get stuck behind a fire truck or held back behind an accident or construction? That's the universe's way of giving you back that negative energy.

> *Whatever you give your attention to, whether positive or negative, you will receive back.*

Contrast that with the times where you're in the least rush: you think that you'll run into traffic so you leave 20 minutes early instead of ten, yet you get there in ten minutes because you're very relaxed about it and not having negative feelings.

Every person is different

What works for me might not work for you. I explain what works for me in this book, but you're not going to be exactly the same. I have techniques and tools throughout the book and in Chapter Ten. You may also find some things that I mention have little effect on you, or can make it worse, or that you don't agree with. That's okay. Brainstorm, Google, try new things, even if it seems silly. Some of my most valued tactics were originally things that I made a write-off. I thought they were embarrassing and stupid and now I do them all the time. At least you'll still have fun in the process and can be able to get a good laugh at yourself. If you can't laugh at yourself, make a joke about doing something silly and be

> *Find small things that work for you!*

comfortable by laughing it off. If something works for you stick with it, no matter how embarrassing you think it may be. If other people see you and if they think it's silly – oh well. Chances are most people that see you doing it will get a good laugh out of it too and they'll laugh with you, not at you. Even if there's no clinical or medical explanation, just go with it. If it doesn't work for you, don't continue with it. Don't keep trying it because it works for your friend or for me. Keep trying and always be looking for new ways to channel and manage your mental health barrier and disability to the best that you can. If you read something, hear something or see something, try it! Never stop trying as persistence and perseverance is the key to overcoming.

8

Make the Three Approaches Work for You

The three approaches are: accept it, change your feelings and perspective and transform. To make the three approaches work or you, engage in self-talk and asking yourself questions to keep you focused on long-term goals. Be easy on yourself. Once you understand yourself you can find things that work for you and be more comfortable in your own shoes. Always practice new things, I have been managing my anxiety since I was a

> *Have an open mind, have fun and even be silly!*

child, and I still look for new and better ways to manage it. I still get caught up in my challenges and anxiety. I still have struggles. Make sure your mind is open to trying new things. Have fun and even be silly. Your energy may rub off and inspire others and it feels really great to be an inspiration and to help others along their own journey.

Set SMART goals

Don't decide that you want your challenges to be conquered overnight and expect it to happen just like that. Each goal you make must have the right steps and path to get there, so set yourself up for success.

Write your goals down and review them daily. I use the online notebook application Evernote to write my goals, see my process and set reminders for myself.

I find that sharing with someone close to me also holds me accountable to my goals and makes me feel more obligated to achieve them. I have some very good business mentors that I work with for this. Having that extra person there that you told that you want to achieve something, that you don't want to let down, that you can show that you did it – can help you achieve your goals. They can be proud of you, give you a little bit of extra motivation and provide guidance.

Practice makes perfect, but perfect doesn't exist so always practice! A bit contradicting but I like to remind myself that there is no such thing as perfect. I just have to keep practicing and working at it. The process is half the battle, it is what makes us who we are and the process makes our entire journey. We shouldn't be living just for the end result. We should be enjoying the journey to those goals.

99% of the time when we set goals they don't go according to plan, which isn't a bad thing … it's life. Often we have to take a different road or maybe fix a pothole to get there. Don't be too serious about achieving your goals exactly by the path you first set because things are going to change. As things change, you can still get to your end result and goal, and enjoy the process – rather than stressing about the result. I can't name one goal I achieved in my life that ever went exactly according to plan. The book, "*The Practicing Mind*" by Thomas M. Sterner, helped me understand about the process versus the product. He talks about how when you focus on the process rather than the product, the process not only goes by quicker, but it's a lot more enjoyable and your goal is much more rewarding.

SMART Goals;

- Specific
- Measurable
- Attainable
- Relevant
- Timely

Here is an example of the SMART goal setting process:

Goal 1 - To eat more vegetables and fruit – healthier body = healthier mind
*Time to achieve – 8 weeks

How am I going to achieve this?

- Eat one serving of fruit with breakfast (an orange or banana)
- Eat one serving of vegetables with both lunch and supper
- Set one reminder at 2:30PM daily in my phone to have one serving of fruit between lunch and supper

Goal 2 - To fall asleep before midnight and sleep for four hours without waking up three nights per week
*Time to achieve – 8 weeks

How am I going to achieve this?

- Practice meditation 10 minutes daily
- Exercise by walking on the treadmill 2 hours prior to going to bed 3 nights per week
- Be laying in bed, reading a book with no TV on at 11pm 3 nights per week

---

Is it SMART? YES! (*Keep a log to measure your results in a journal, your phone or somewhere else that is easily accessible that you will see every day.*)

Notice how I started small by one piece at a time with a timeline of 8 weeks? Once you achieve your SMART goals, you can just keep setting and making larger goals! It may seem small but that sets you up for success. Chances are you may even achieve it sooner and then set more goals once you start feeling good with your goal setting system and success.

Choose over what do you want more or what do you want now?

When I struggle with self-discipline or my follow-through, I ask myself, "what do I want now or what do I want more?" 99% of the time what I want now is impulse that negatively influences what I want more and my goals, so I don't make the impulse decision. Most people don't stop to ask themselves this and they just go with what they're wanting now.

You will be surprised at how easy implementing what you really want is as soon as you ask yourself the question and give yourself time to answer. Most of the time when I ask myself, "what do I want now or what do I want more?" I end up realizing that I want something else more. The thought of what I want more prevents me from making those decisions about the now that are short sighted and do not benefit my long-tem goals.

> *Ask yourself, "What do I want now or what do I want more?"*

Realize that everything that you do is a choice: how you feel, how you act, how you react. It is all a choice.

Take the time to ask yourself the question and think about your answer. Most things aren't good rushed. With mental health barriers and disabilities, it's important to process what we're thinking or contemplating. Most of the time we act on things before we have an opportunity to think about them. Our brains may be working faster than we can keep up with, so we just act the way that our brains tell us to without stepping back and thinking and processing what we're doing. I have been guilty of that and I used to be *very* impulsive. Now I've gained the practice of when I feel impulsive or emotional, I pull myself out of the situation, step back and ask myself what I am really feeling at this moment and what I can do about it.

One of the biggest parts of overcoming a mental health barrier and disability is processing things in your mind logically. Sometimes our minds seem to go off on their own without us even noticing. Once we do notice, it's too late to stop an impulse decision. Learning how to slow things down and process them is vital – which is why being aware and understanding your mental health and disability makes a world of a difference. If you're not self-aware, you don't understand and you can't make different decisions.

Some examples of scenarios when I ask myself "What do I want now and what do I want more?" are:

- Eating unhealthy - What I want now is a chocolate bar. What I want more is to live a healthy lifestyle without eating sugar and chocolate.

- Doing tasks and prioritizing – What I want now is to surf on the internet or waste time on FaceBook. What I want more is to achieve my goals with my career and mental health.

- Physiotherapy and exercise – What I want now is to not be in pain during a session and to skip my appointment or gym time. What I want more is do have better pain management and manage my chronic pain long-term.

- Purchases – What I want now is to buy that article of clothing, or souvenir that I may only use once. What I want more is to save money and spend it on things that I need or will use more often.

- Watching TV – What I want now is to watch TV and lay on the couch. What I want more is to get my work done or go outside and take my dog for a walk.

- Relationships conflict – What I want now is to be frustrated and not talk. What I want more is to be happy and sort through any disagreements and conflict and have good communication

Self-talk

This is something that I do that I thought was really silly at first and if other people saw me doing it they would look at me really weird – but it happens to be one of the things that works the most for me. Self-talk, as we are describing here, is telling yourself something *out loud* to make yourself feel good about what you're <u>currently</u> doing and where you are in your life, embracing the present (*not the future*). This is called a declaration. Our brains think, but they don't often have time to actually hear our thoughts so when we say our thoughts out loud we can actually process them. We want to do declarations, not affirmations.

Affirmations are when we tell ourselves we have achieved our goals in a future tense – which actually make us feel worse about ourselves because we are not there yet.

Self-talk is important for anyone. Whether it's self-talk about your goals, how you feel about yourself or whether it's getting over a situation and calming yourself down from anxiety, it helps you process what you're thinking by saying it out loud to yourself. However, it can also work against

> *Be sure to make yourself feel good about the things that you say to yourself!*

you and put you under too much pressure if you don't do it properly. I do declarations daily in the morning and before I go to bed in the mirror. It's important to believe the things that you're saying to yourself, or it can have a reverse effect on your feelings.

What is the difference between declarations and affirmations?

Self-talk as we are describing here is telling yourself something out loud to make yourself feel good about what you're <u>currently</u> doing and where you are in your life, embracing the present (not the future), so you can hear yourself say it.

Affirmations are telling yourself lies in a future tense regarding your goals, which can actually make you feel worse about yourself because you are not there yet.

Examples of self-talk statements that are declarations:

- I am on the road to having less anxiety

- I have set myself up for success for my goals

- I feel good about my choices

- I am learning to be more accepting of my mental health challenges and disabilities

- I have been eating healthier and am on the road to living a better lifestyle

- I have done a great job of learning about my mental health and disability which helps me work at overcoming it

- I have a great plan and am working hard to overcome my challenges

Examples of affirmations that are not present achievements:

- I don't have Tourette's Syndrome

- I am famous

- I am rich

- I have lost 50 pounds

- I have my dream career

- I am not depressed (If you do struggle with depression)

Transforming is an everlasting journey

Never give up on yourself. You will always be finding out more about yourself and growing as an individual and it's really exciting to get to know yourself and who you really are once you stop hiding. Look forward to defining a stronger you. Enjoy the ride and the process of reaching your goals and don't focus on the result or product. Focus on the things that are going well and that will give you strength to pull through hardships. When you're having a tough time, remind yourself of the positive. Give yourself credit for the small things and most importantly, don't forget to love yourself!

> *It's a great thing that this will likely be with you for the rest of your life, find how to take advantage of that!*

9

Paying It Forward

It's important to pay your good feelings, passion and knowledge forward to others. Most people in our society don't do this because they're so wrapped up in their own lives in the new age of remote careers and communication. Technology has made the personal touch not so personal anymore. By paying it forward, you stand out and get recognized as a kind, great and happy person. My clients, friends and associates say that I'm always smiling and they can't help but smile when being around me. It's contagious.

> *Take the extra time for someone, it's quite an amazing feeling!*

When others want to feel better, they reach out to me. Having others trust and confide in me – it is an irreplaceable feeling. I have found that even if I am having a tough time, when somebody reaches out to me for help, it can turn my attitude around too.

How can you pay it forward?

- Be kind to others

- Help a stranger carry groceries

- Hold a door for somebody

- Smile at somebody

- Say hi to someone new

- Volunteer for a non-profit organization with a great cause

- Phone someone - just because you want to reach out

- Spread good news

- Bring someone a cup of coffee or tea

- Listen to others

- Provide encouraging words to others

- Ask how someone's day is

- Say thank you

- Be polite

- Help someone through a rough time – just be there for them

- Compliment others

- Let someone in your traffic lane

Bullying

You never know what somebody else's situation is. Others could be having a rough day which you could make or break, so choose to make it. People may have rough home lives, work lives, health

Normally the bullies are the ones that are bullied the most!

problems, mental health problems, even a death of somebody they know – which we must be mindful of.

Normally the bullies are the bullied. The worst bullies are often the ones that are bullied the most.

It feels great to make other people smile. If you're having a bad day and someone else smiled at you, said hi and asked about your day and listened for a few seconds, it could make your day. Do that for others. Don't pay it forward to get something out of it, do it because it provides you with internal happiness. That's all you need out of it.

The Golden Rule and Law of Attraction

In elementary school, we all learned about the Golden Rule. To treat others how you want to be treated. You never know somebody else's situation, and it feels great to be a good person and the bigger person when situations require it. Some people with their own insecurities tend not to be the bigger person and you may struggle to be the bigger person in those situations. But if you can achieve that, it feels really great. During conflict, it can be one of the hardest things in the world to do.

In earlier chapters I discussed the law of attraction in which you will get back what you receive – whether positive or negative – so if you're putting positive out to people you're going to get positive back and if you're putting negative out to people you're going to get negative back. I truly believe that what you give is what you get.

> *What you give is what you get whether positive or negative!*

Be a good listener. Remember people and what's important to them. People want to feel heard, sometimes it's just nice to have someone listen and not say anything.

Be honest with people about who you are. Don't lie. Just be the best person that you can be every day.

Gratitude

Express gratitude and be thankful every day. It's important to be thankful for things that we have and express our gratitude. I am so blessed. We can often forget that we have a roof over our head, food on the table, clothes on our back. We should be thankful for those things. We tend to get accustomed to our daily routines when they become expectations, we can lose our gratitude toward blessings like food in our fridge and having meals to eat, spending time with our family and friends, or a warm bed to sleep in.

Keep a gratitude journal. Every day I write down something that I'm thankful for. It could be the smallest thing. I have so much to be thankful for that every day I can write something new. Most of us focus on a small percentage of the things that aren't going our way and dwell on them. Earlier in the book, I mentioned the 90/10 rule in the book, *"Focus on the 90%" by Darci Lang*. We tend to focus on the 10% of things that aren't going well in our lives. When we do this, we forget to be thankful and appreciative for what we have. Don't take life for granted.

We have a great life, even with the negative things that are happening to us. It all happens for a reason; the challenges and the obstacles that we encounter are just life's way of trying to help us grow. Each day is a

Find something to be thankful for every day!

new day, if you don't do something right today you have tomorrow to do it better. Life is very forgiving and it's never too late.

What can we be thankful for?

- Other kind individuals
- Our dog, cats and other pets – If you don't have any, the SPCA always takes visitors and volunteers
- Our family and friends
- Our jobs
- Food on the table
- A roof over our heads
- Sleep
- Heat in the winter
- Good health
- Money
- Weekends
- Learning from mistakes
- Reading books
- Laughter
- Safety and security
- Technology
- Freedom of speech and religion
- Art
- Music
- Sunshine
- Our five senses
- Nature
- Architecture
- Entertainment

The smallest things make the biggest difference

Helping others helps me and the smallest things make the biggest difference. Those teeny tiny little efforts could make another person's entire day. I love making another person's day. It boosts my day up that much more too. It feels great to be known for happiness, smiling and optimism, knowing that people trust me. Helping others will help me grow.

10

Techniques and Tools

Finding the right management techniques and tools can be difficult. Here are some techniques and tools to help you get started!

1. Managing anxiety with relaxation:

- Do small things
- Go for a walk or to the gym for exercise
- Have a cup of tea
- Listen to music
- Dance around the house with a broom as you clean
- Light candles and relax on your couch or bed
- Color, doodle or paint… something artsy that brings out your artist
- Watch cartoons
- Burn lavender essential oils
- Meditate
- Listen to Mozart

- Have a bath
- Don't try to fight or give yourself a hard time. *(All you need to do is say, "Okay, I accept my anxiety and I'm not going to try to fight it." When you fight your anxiety it makes it a hundred times worse than it needs to be. Accept it and move on from it. Don't try to reason with yourself because when we have anxiety, there's no purpose or reasoning)*

2. Focusing with ADD and ADHD

- Turn your phone on silent during tasks
- Take a 10 or 15 minute break to stretch or read after a task to refresh your mind
- Stop multitasking
- Find a task management software and prioritize *(I use Evernote and a software called Todoist for this)*
- Have a To Do list
- Make your To Do list the night before so you can think about what you've got to do. Wake up, look at your list, organize it and then do the tasks

3. Calm Panic attacks

- Know to recognize one
- Talk out loud, focus on and control your breathing. *(I lay on my back, I put my hands on my stomach and I stomach breathe – pushing my stomach out really big and expanding my diaphragm without moving my chest.)* Most people breathe and expand their chest, which doesn't help calm panic attacks. Put your hands on your stomach, breathe in and out, in and out. With your hands still on your stomach count from one to ten and ten down to one. Each breath out should be 8 times longer than your breath in. By the time that you've counted down to one, your anxiety or panic attack is calmed down quite a

bit – if not gone. *(I like to pretend that my stomach is waves of the ocean as well.)*

- Get some fresh air.

- Find something to bring you back to reality and ground you, like objects in the room. Feel your pen, feel your mouse, feel your fork, feel whatever you need to feel so you can bring yourself back down to reality.

- Ask yourself what is real, and don't try to fight or give yourself a hard time. Every time that we have panic attacks we know that we're having a panic attack and we say, "Oh my gosh, I'm panicking for no reason". We all know it, but we can't stop it.

- Keep a diary on your attacks to refer back to.

- Stay away from caffeine, cigarettes, alcohol and drugs. These things severally increase your anxiety. I have not had any kind of caffeine *(even a coffee)* in over five years. I don't smoke, I don't do alcohol or drugs at all. Period. I feel great. If I do have a glass of wine with supper, I get a bit of anxiety – so I rarely even do that. I probably have one glass of wine with supper once every three months and then realize I don't want to do it again anytime soon because it makes me feel awful and anxious.

4. Dial Back Depression

- First of all accept that you're depressed and don't try to fake being happy. It's okay to be depressed. Nothing's wrong with you.

- Cuddle with a pet or a teddy bear

- Eat something healthy like a salad so you don't feel guilty about gorging yourself or eating unhealthily.

- Ask someone for help, even if it's just to be there beside you or cuddling

- Write it down, sometimes it feels good to get it out on paper

- Find a support group.

- Don't try to make yourself somebody that you're not and don't try to force yourself out of depression when you just can't.

5. Learning something new with ADHD, ADD or a learning disability

- Try to figure out how you learn and the way that you learn best. For example, I'm not an auditory or a visual learner. I'm a hands-on learner, I need to see it and do it myself so when I'm stuck in any kind of lecture or meeting where I can't write as fast as the speaking I use a voice recorder. Then I can refer back to the lecturer or I ask for it to be explained in a different way. I'll simply say, "I don't fully understand, can you please explain that in a different way, or can you please elaborate?"

- I make notes during the class or I'll ask, "Can you show me?"

- Get help with your cognitive functioning through schoolwork or the Learning Disability Association. I've done neurofeedback, which is cognitive brain training through the Learning Disability Association and it made a world of a difference for me. It's not free of charge, but it definitely does help.

6. Reverse the Negative Thinking

- The Elastic Band Trick. It's a 30 day challenge to yourself. Put an elastic band around your wrist and catch yourself with thinking negative. When the negative thoughts happen, snap the elastic band to the point where it hurts. The psychology behind this is that out of all of the emotions and all the neurotransmitters and signals, your brain remembers pain the most because it wants to protect itself against getting hurt. So when you snap the elastic band it causes you pain. Your brain recognizes it and tries to prevent future situations that are going to cause you pain. Your brain will prevent you from being negative because it's been causing you pain. *(It actually worked quite well for me, but I was very consistent with it. I was regular with snapping the band when I thought negative).*

• Keep a gratitude journal of the things that you're thankful for and when you're feeling negative go over it. Every day write something that you're thankful for and then remind yourself when you're negative of all those things.

• I've started a positive attribute list about myself, these are the things that I'm comfortable with and I love about myself. The list grows as time goes on but it started very small. This is a non-physical list such as; my organization, my ability to never give up, my perseverance, my passion, and my kindness. Make a positive attribute list about yourself and read it over when you're thinking negative. Have it handy on your phone or somewhere where you're going to be able to reach for it.

• Do declarations, those are the things that you say to yourself out loud that make you feel good about your goals.

• Make a list of any of the small things that you've achieved, that 10% of things I was talking about before that we forget to give ourselves credit for. Look at that 10% that you don't give yourself the credit for and go, "Oh, I actually did several things today."

7. Fighting hypochondria.

• We all know that hypochondria is one of the most outrageously unreasonable irrational things we may have. I used to have it really bad when I was 14 or 15. I got over it when I was 18 or 19 to the point where it no longer impaired my thinking and my actions. I no longer visited the doctor for unnecessary worry. I got over it thanks to counselling, my father's support and having a much healthier lifestyle with exercise and nutrition. Since I have been over it, I have my yearly check up with my doctor and dentist, but that's pretty much it. I am not irrational about those types of thoughts about my well being anymore – even though I still really suffer from generalized anxiety.

- **DO NOT Google it!!**! Accept that you're worrying and go do something to take your mind off of it. When you Google it you come up with 18 different things that it, actually could be based on internet symptoms.

- Get somebody close to you to tell you that you're being silly and that what you're saying is not possible. Oftentimes I had to get my dad to say, "Brett, you're being silly, that's not possible and it's not going to happen." As soon as I have somebody tell me that I'm being silly, the irrational thought usually goes away.

- Ask yourself, "Has anything that I've ever worried about actually happened to me?" The answer 99.9% of the time, no. And then you say, "Well, but what if it happens to me this time?" No, it's just like every other time where nothing's actually wrong.

- Do something to make yourself feel better, like have a bath, go for a walk, get yourself busy, find something around the house to do, exercise, talk to someone – do anything but dwell on the idea.

- Just relax, don't overthink it which is one of the hardest things to do. Remind yourself that it's your anxiety.

These are just a few things that I have tried myself, there is an endless possibility of techniques and tools. If you don't find any items that work for you or a loved one on my list, don't give up and keep trying because there will be things that work.

11

The End of the Story

Thank you for reading my book, I hope that this book has provided you with inspiration, education and a new perspective whether you're struggling yourself with mental health and disabilities or you have a loved one that struggles.

The truth is, having a mental health or disability does not mean that you're broken. It's all about your perspective, it makes you exceptional and it *can* be used as a strength.

It's now your time to shine! Turn things around for yourself and rock your mental health and disabilities. If you have a loved one that struggles, inspire and support them to do the same.

So you've got Tourette's? – Awesome!

How about anxiety? – Great!

ADHD? – Right on!

RESOURCES

Books:

Focus on the 90% by Darci Lang

The Practicing Mind by Thomas M. Sterner

The Law of Attraction by Esther and Jerry Hicks

Websites:

http://themighty.com/2016/04/letter-to-people-who-think-chronic-pain-isnt-that-bad/

http://www.huffingtonpost.com/2014/11/13/mental-illness-physical-i_n_6145156.html

Associations:

Mental Health Association of America -

www.mentalhealthamerica.net/

Canadian Mental Health Association -

www.cmha.ca

AUTHOR SERVICES

Want to bring Brett in for an event? How about listen to her radio show, watch her TV series or get some mental health clothing?

Brett Provides Professional Speaking such as:

- Keynotes

- Interpersonal Seminars

- Workplace Mental Health (Presenting, consulting and strategizing)

- Individual Coaching Sessions

Not only that, but Brett is also an expert in helping children of all ages (from the youngest to teenagers) with their healthy development, living with challenges, and assisting their parents in understanding them better.

IMPORTANT: All of the Brett's event topics are very customizable. Whether it's a banquet, conference, school/college, corporate event, seminar, training or other, we will work with you to ensure we achieve your goals. You choose from many options to create an awesome program tailored to your specific event.

Brett's presentations are guaranteed to engage your audience!

Not Broken® Radio

Brett's weekly radio show is aimed towards having open and honest discussion about mental health.

Check it out at www.notbrokenradio.com

Not Broken® Clothing

Brett's mental health clothing line provokes an open and honest discussion about mental health with a goal of stopping the stigma, educating others and inspiring those struggling to feel comfortable in their own shoes.

Shop her clothing at www.urnotbroken.ca

Breaking The Barriers TV Series

Brett continues to work on a TV series called "Breaking the Barriers!" It is syndicated across the nation. It's a TV series to create more mental health and disability awareness and education. Brett is passionate about inspiring people to overcome these barriers and helping them realize that having a mental health barrier or disability makes them an exceptional individual, they are not broken!

Check it out at www.brettfrancis.ca

See www.brettfrancis.ca to learn more about her services and to listen to her radio show or watch her TV series!

CONTACT INFO

Brett Francis

Professional Speaker
Host
Author
Producer
Coach

Toll Free 855.910.8255
Fax 855.759.5221
admin@francisventures.ca
www.brettfrancis.ca

AUTHOR BIOGRAPHY

Do you have Tourette's? Awesome! How about anxiety? Great! Depression? So what?! ADHD, OCD? Right on!

Brett Francis is a professional speaker and mental health advocate, with a TV and radio show. - Her radio show, Not Broken® Radio has 1.8M+ listeners/downloads per month. She's also a best selling author and has a mental health clothing line, all aimed towards having open and honest discussion about mental health and disabilities and also to give confidence to those struggling.

There was once a little girl, only 6 years old, who was diagnosed with Tourette's Syndrome and severe ADHD. This caused her to struggle through the entirety of her school years with not only her grades but also with being bullied harshly, unable to even turn to her family who didn't understand her, and no matter what she tried (and she did!) to fit in, however she attempted to change herself, all she ended up with was severe depression, the lingering thoughts of feeling broken, wondering what was wrong with her, and medications for over eleven years.

When she was 17 years old, she was also diagnosed with anxiety, OCD and panic disorder. This has caused her to encounter many barriers as she grew into an adult and became a business woman.

Then, in 2012, this young woman was involved in two serious motor vehicle accidents. She was off from work for almost 1 full year because of the injuries she suffered, and is living with chronic pain ever since. Yet, despite these injuries, she pushed on, and came out stronger than ever.

Then, in 2012, this young woman was involved in two serious motor vehicle accidents. She was off from work for almost 1 full year because of the injuries she suffered, and is living with chronic pain ever since. Yet, despite these injuries, she pushed on, and came out stronger than ever.

She's here to tell you what you probably already know: stories like that are sadly not as unique as we'd like to think. I'd also like to tell you that it's not a disadvantage, and definitely not the end of the line or a life sentence.

"From the first time I met with Brett her passion for advocating for persons living with mental health diagnoses was evident. Her passion for breaking down barriers for those in similar shoes encouraged me to invite her to speak at the Canadian Council on Rehabilitation and Work (CCRW)'s annual Business Awards Luncheon this year. Her dedication to the idea of equality is contagious, and her story touched everyone that was in attendance – some of our clients even pulled me aside after the event to thank me for finding such a motivational and fantastic guest speaker such as Brett! I would encourage anyone and everyone to book Brett as your next guest speaker for any and all future events, you will definitely not be disappointed!"
Sarah - Canadian Council on Rehabilitation and Work

Fact is, everyone is able to forge experiences like that into strengths and personal power, even if they don't know it yet. This may be you, your loved ones, your friends or co-workers, since the solution isn't something that needs any particular talent. It's a philosophy. A state of mind.

It can not only shape your life, but it will also help others in theirs. Her philosophy involves three simple approaches that has helped her and many others in overcoming mental health barriers, disabilities, anxiety and stress, difficulties in business, entrepreneurship, relationships, life and health! Working with Brett helps you embrace your true self and feel empowered about it! Her work with individuals, groups, associations and businesses makes them understand and work through mental health barriers.

She has a simple, uplifting and refreshing style that helps many transform how they feel about themselves and their struggles. She's faced many challenges with anxiety, disabilities, life and businesses, and yet (or exactly because of it!) she came out on top as a strong business woman, the proud Owner, CEO and President of multiple companies. She's constantly learning and is passionate about expanding my knowledge.

There is one simple thing she'd like everyone to understand: you are not broken. She spent a lot of her life feeling broken and has dedicated her life to making sure not only you, but every single person understands this very baseline truth. Misconceptions, lackluster education and the lack of general awareness had created a stigma, but the person that can fight it? It's you. Maybe you already are, maybe you just want to, but one thing is certain: you can. She is, as plenty of others, every single day of their lives, with or without disabilities of their own, and the thing that binds it all together? The realization that challenge and disability doesn't equal disadvantage.

Recall that little girl I told you about? Brett is that girl. She lived to learn that virtually nothing has to be disabling and has activated a power that she may not have found without those experiences. Now she shares her empowerment and experiences to educate others, stop the stigma and give others struggling confidence in their own challenges. Having a mental health challenge or disability does not mean that we are broken.

"Brett is a professional speaker and an entrepreneur. She has written a book, records a radio show, and is really freaking strong (just look at her arms!). Brett also has Tourette syndrome and first hand experience working through other mental illnesses.
And she says "that's great!"

Last night, the Business & Professional Women hosted an amazing event, with inspiring women spreading important messages. The thing about important messages is that they need to be shared. Not just by the people who were a part of the story, but by people who have heard the story. And the story I heard last night about celebrating mental illness is one that needs to be shared.

Say what now? Isn't mental illness this terribly, horrible, dark and scary thing that we want to avoid at all cost? After all, even Clara Hughes admits on her website that she couldn't bring herself to tell her own mother about her depression (her Mom found out from T.V.) because she didn't want it to be a burden.

So, why should we celebrate something that is such a burden? Well...

Who says it's a burden? - What makes it a burden? - Who says it's not a good thing? - How can mental illness possibly be a good thing? - Is there anything in your life that you've been able to say, or do, or feel, or express - because you have a mental illness? - Maybe you're able to empathize with others on a deep and genuine level. - Maybe you are very in tuned with how others are feeling. - Maybe you developed a sense of strength. - Maybe you've written a book or a blog. - Maybe you've been able to share your story with 1 other person who now has hope because of you.

Those are just a few of the reasons why mental illness is worth celebrating.

I came away from last night looking at mental illness with a different lens. A positive lens. And although it doesn't feel quite right say that yet (it's a huge shift in mindset!), it also feels very right.

To all my friends who are struggling and triumphing as you read this. Right on! You are who you are, and I love you for it - not in spite of your mental illness, but because of it."

Kelly - Disrupt HR

Through professional speaking, hosting her TV and radio show, writing her book, providing seminars and coaching, creating her mental health clothing line, Brett has inspired thousands of people dealing with struggles to fit in, feel "normal", and overcome the barriers in their lives by rocking their challenges.

Just as an example, here are her three most popular topics:

"The invisible woman unlocking the unique power of misunderstood people with mental health challenges and disabilities"

"They see me but they don't really see me" - This topic is tailored to all audiences whether they are people who live with these challenges themselves, or it's their loved ones, co-workers, bosses, and even people who don't have any personal or family experiences with mental health issues and disabilities.

She likes to focus on general understanding, correcting misconceptions and teaching people how to talk about it and side-step the stigma. Turning disabilities into "abilities" and how we can embrace our challenges and use them to our advantage! She likes to do this in a fun and light-hearted way because people are less awkward and more inclined to be involved.

"The things we know but do not say - Love languages of mental health challenges and disabilities"
Understanding others with mental health challenges and disabilities.

"Is everyone here crazy? - Managing mental health in the workplace"
Each speech/seminar targets very important levels within an organization that can have a major impact on people suffering with mental health conditions as well as severe corporate/organizational economic loss.

Brett has been active in the business community for a number of years and have been involved in several other successful business ventures. She has a deep understanding of what it takes to be successful in business. As previous VP, VP of Sales and Marketing, other executive positions with large corporations, among other great ventures and experiences, she possesses strong entrepreneurial skills and knowledge to not only move forward with new business ventures, but to make them a great success! She brings abundant energy, drive to succeed, dedication, passion and integrity to everything that she does!

She's an active member in the community and currently involves herself with many things such as working with disabled, volunteering and fundraising as part of a number of mental health organizations and has been involved with many other causes and non-profit organizations in the last decade. She's also endorsed by mental health associations across the globe as a Mental Health Advocate, including but not limited to: Mental Health America and Canadian Mental Health Foundation, and am Mental Health First Aid Certified.

She shares her life experiences in my presentations from her struggles in school, with jobs, money, relationships, self-confidence, anxiety, disabilities all the way through to growing her own successful businesses from ground up, starting from nothing.

She started her first company when she was 22 years old. How? She practices her simple philosophy to overcome numerous barriers every single day.